FRED CLAIRE

My 30 Years in Dodger Blue

FRED CLAIRE

WITH

STEVE SPRINGER

FOREWORD BY OREL HERSHISER

WWW.SPORTSPUBLISHINGLLC.COM

Director of production: Susan M. Moyer
Project manager: Greg Hickman
Developmental editor: Gabe Rosen
Photo editor: Erin Linden-Levy
Dust jacket design: Joseph Brumleve
Copy editor: Holly Birch

ISBN: 1-58261-732-5

Printed in the United States.

*Hall of Fame catcher and friend Roy Campanella
visits with Fred in spring training.*

CONTENTS

INTRODUCTION

They were America's team long before the Dallas Cowboys.

They were loved at first because of their charming ineptness, the lovable bums who gained the sympathy of a nation.

Then they were supported for their fairness and boldness, the team that broke the color barrier and helped launch the civil rights movement.

And finally, they were cheered and respected for their success, the perennial pennant winners who finally won a world championship in 1955. And it was all the sweeter because, in doing so, they beat their constant tormentors, the New York Yankees.

They were the Brooklyn Dodgers, a team so well known that many of its stars needed only a nickname—Duke, Newk, Pee Wee, Campy, Oisk, Preacher, The Barber—to be identified.

They were the stuff of legends, the club that could boast of a Jackie Robinson and smile at a Babe Herman, the team that rose above racism and was felled by the shot heard 'round the world.

America couldn't seem to get enough of the Brooklyn Dodgers.

But then in 1958, it all ended, badly and sadly for the borough of Brooklyn. Its beloved Dodgers went west and the only ball Ebbets Field had in front of it was a wrecking ball.

That may have been the last chapter of the Brooklyn Dodger saga, but there was still a great sequel ahead.

The story of the Los Angeles Dodgers has also been one of drama and color. They were the trailblazers who opened up the western half of this country for baseball in particular, and sports in general, playing at first in front of Coliseum crowds three times larger than the capacity of Ebbets. And then they moved into Dodger Stadium, which has maintained its inspiring atmosphere and flawless beauty for more than four decades.

There were Sandy and Maury, Big D and Little D, Fernandomania and Nomomania, Bulldog, Gibson, Piazza and Karros right up to Green and Gagne, big stars producing big moments, generating record-setting attendance figures and achieving more success than the Brooklyn Dodgers ever enjoyed. The team has won five world championships in Los Angeles. Three Hall of Famers—Sandy Koufax, Don Drysdale and Don Sutton—had their prime years in L.A., as did two Hall of Fame managers, Walter Alston and Tommy Lasorda.

The L.A. Dodgers have carved their own niche in baseball history. Koufax put together arguably the best five-year stretch of pitching by any individual. Fernando Valenzuela became an international phenomenon. Kirk Gibson hit one of baseball's most memorable home runs. Maury Wills revolutionized the game by making the stolen base once again an offensive weapon. And Eric Gagne is threatening to again revolutionize the game by making the ninth inning off-limits to opposing clubs.

The Dodgers never stopped being America's team. They just switched coasts.

Even off the field, the team has remained in the national spotlight. The selling of the Dodgers, the last Mom-and-Pop operation in baseball under the O'Malleys, to corporate giant Fox shook up the industry.

And now, it has come full circle with the announcement by Fox that it plans to sell the team.

The Fox era alone is a fascinating story.

Yet surprisingly, neither this story nor so many others of the L.A. era have been adequately told. There have been few in-depth books about the inner workings of the Los Angeles Dodgers.

The reason is twofold. Few have lived through it on the inside, and none of those who did were willing to share their experiences.

That is no longer the case with the publication of this book by Fred Claire, who is uniquely qualified to bring the Dodger story up to date.

He spent 30 years in the Dodger front office and several years before that covering the team as a sportswriter.

Two of the most momentous events of those years served as bookends to Claire's career as general manager. He got the job when Al Campanis was fired and lost it as a result of the Mike Piazza trade, a trade he publicly conceded was made without his prior knowledge by a Fox executive.

With the departure of Fox, Claire's story finally has an ending.

I wanted to be part of this project because I think it is a necessary and worthwhile endeavor, producing the newest chapters in the story of this colorful and enduring franchise, a story that stretches back over more than a century from the Brooklyn Dodgers of 1890 to the Los Angeles Dodgers of the 21st Century.

Fred Claire was there for three of those decades. And hopefully, after you read this book, you will feel like you were there as well.

Steve Springer

ACKNOWLEDGMENTS

I couldn't have written this book, wouldn't have written it, without the support and encouragement of my family.

The job of a general manager is no different than any other job in one respect: It is the people we come home to who mean the most to us.

My wife Sheryl was always there with me during my years as the Dodger GM. Her support and encouragement never wavered.

In 30 years with the team, I devoted most of my time and energy to the organization. There were occasions when it was at the expense of time with my children—Jeff, Jennifer and Kim. People in baseball and in all businesses understand these decisions. I wish to acknowledge the love and support I have received from my children. They are adults now with achievements of their own, and they know how proud I am of them.

The Dodgers were a big part of my life for many years. The people who served the organization—from clubhouse workers to players, from ushers to department heads—will probably never know how much they have meant to me.

There are so many friends from all walks of life who have given me encouragement through the years. Indeed, there are people who I don't even know who have reached out to provide words that have inspired me.

I had all but given up the thought of writing this book when I received a telephone call one day from Steve Springer. He asked a pointed question: "Fred, have you ever thought of doing a book?"

I'm sure there have been times when Steve wishes he hadn't posed the question. It ultimately produced a great deal of work for him, but he handled it in a manner that reflected the professional he is.

There is no real way to single out individuals who have impacted my life. I can only hope that those people who know me also know how much I care for them.

Fred Claire

FOREWORD

Because I spent most of my career with the Dodgers, reporters would come to me to find out what it was like to play for a family-owned team, where tradition was honored and integrity was sacred, where a man's simple word was his bond. I was always happy to tell them about the legacy of the O'Malley family, how it felt to work for people of impeccable character. I would also tell them about Fred Claire.

As you'll discover in this terrific book, Fred loves baseball. Sure, he was a businessman—and a very good one at that—but mostly, his focus has always been on the game. As a small boy in rural Ohio, Fred would often be taken by his parents, along with his brother and sister, to old Crosley Field to watch the Reds. The experience was bigger than life, leaving young Fred filled with a passion for baseball that, he admits, has never left him.

In 1969, Fred joined the Dodgers as the team's director of publicity. At that time, I was an 11-year-old Little Leaguer, thousands of miles from Southern California, learning how to play the game. Fifteen years later, I got the call every aspiring youngster dreams of—the invitation to the majors.

It was then that I first met Fred Claire. I remember being impressed with his kindness toward this rookie and his genuine interest in my life. In a world where strong egos and self-interest were the rule, Fred was the exception, a humble man, far more interested in me than himself.

"How's Jamie?" he'd ask about my wife when he'd see me in the clubhouse. He knew that Jamie had left her family in Texas in order to join me in Los Angeles. He knew of the adjustments involved in being married to a big leaguer. And Fred truly cared. Long before my career catapulted me to the front page of the sports section, Fred helped us find a home in Pasadena. This was a man with a good heart. And Jamie and I knew it.

Four years after my arrival, Fred moved to the front office as the Dodgers' general manager. A year later, we were sporting our new World Series rings, on top of the world.

During the offseason that followed, the Dodgers made me the highest paid player in the history of the game. The contract negotiations gave me a deeper look into the character of Fred Claire. Fred was determined to keep those negotiations out of the paper. And that he did, handling them in a classy manner. I was so appreciative of that.

With the whole sports world examining his every move, Fred was always measured. Careful. The complete professional, he was never arrogant or self-absorbed. Although a tireless competitor who thrilled at the Dodgers' success, Fred refused to stand in the limelight. In fact, he used the moment of Dodger glory in '88 to connect us with those who had gone before us: Johnny Podres, Sandy Koufax, Larry Sherry, Carl Erskine, Roy Campanella and Don Drysdale. A man who cherished the Dodger pedigree, Fred wanted us to feel the responsibility of carrying on that heritage with the same distinction.

And during a time when we could have been consumed with ourselves, Fred didn't let us forget our responsibility to serve the greater community.

Although players rarely talk about it, there is sometimes a feeling that the front office controls your life. But as a player, I trusted Fred's truthfulness and good judgment. This gave me the freedom to focus on my own performance without uncertainty or fear creeping in.

It felt good to play for a team like that. Even on the day in 1994 when Fred told me there was no future for me with the Dodgers.

It was unseasonably cold the morning I drove from my Pasadena home to Chavez Ravine. A meeting had been scheduled with Fred and Peter O'Malley to discuss my contract situation. Robert Fraley, my representative, had offered to come along, but I was completely confident in my relationship with these men. So I went alone.

Rosie Gutierrez, Fred's assistant, greeted me and then beeped her boss. "Orel's here to see you and Mr. O'Malley," she informed them.

Fred and Peter stood and greeted me warmly as I walked into an adjoining office, then we sat down in the comfortable chairs surrounding the coffee table. After a few minutes of catching up on how the offseason had been going, Fred dove in. He asked about my intentions for the future. He asked what I wanted to do for the 1995 season. I told him that I felt strong and wanted to continue to pitch. With the same gracious spirit I had come to appreciate, Fred let me know that he didn't think that there would be an opportunity for me to continue to do that with the Dodgers. They weren't sure that I'd have much more to contribute at 36.

I told Fred and Mr. O'Malley that, because of the ongoing lockout situation, they had not been able to see me practice. But I assured them that I was throwing as well as ever and knew that I could still get big-league hitters out. I wasn't ready to quit.

*Opening day, 1989, Fred is honored as Executive of the Year
and Orel Hershiser as Cy Young Award winner.*

They understood and wished me well. (By the way, I went on to win 70 more games in the big leagues. Nobody claimed that Fred was perfect.)

As I left the meeting, I remember how I felt. I was disappointed, for sure. But I was not angry. I was sincerely grateful to the Dodgers. And I was thankful for these men and nothing was going to change that.

Still, Peter and Fred, as courteous as they had been, *were* businessmen and had to make the call as they saw it. I understood.

That could have easily been the end of my friendship with Fred Claire, but it wasn't. I have continued to stay in touch with him. Believing that after my retirement—which happened five years later—I'd continue to be involved in some facet of the game, I wanted to put into practice the things I had learned from him and I wanted to continue to learn from him. Fred had taught me how to carry myself as a baseball executive. A professional. I had seen him exhibit that poise in various settings, from standing at a podium in front of a bank of microphones to greeting fans in a hotel lobby. Although he had never been a coach or manager like Tommy Lasorda, Ron Perranoski, Bobby Valentine or Dusty Baker, his influence was no less important to me than that gleaned from some of the greatest in the game.

Although you will probably never know Fred Claire as I know him, you can completely trust what he is about to tell you in this book. His character is thoroughly consistent with his word. As a role model for me, Fred has proven himself worthy to be an example and a teacher.

For this, I will always be grateful.

Orel Hershiser
Dallas, Texas

CHAPTER I

THE END

It began as one of the saddest days of my 30 years in Dodger blue, but I never dreamed it would deteriorate further, ending as my last day in Dodger blue.

It was Father's Day, June 21, 1998, a family day, but, as the general manager of the Dodgers, I felt an obligation to be with the team whenever possible. And so there I was on that Sunday, in a visiting suite at Denver's Coors Field, watching from above as the Dodgers concluded a series against the Colorado Rockies.

It hadn't been an easy trip. Or an easy season. The trading a month earlier of catcher Mike Piazza, one of the most popular players in team history, had sent shock waves through the organization that would reverberate for years to come.

I was trying to stabilize a very shaky situation. When a general manager makes a bad trade, his spirit is damaged. When a trade is made without the knowledge of the general manager, his credibility is shattered.

When I learned after the fact from team president Bob Graziano that Piazza had been sent to the Florida Marlins as part of a seven-player deal, I decided to resign. But Graziano and Fox executive Chase Carey assured me the Piazza deal was an aberration, that I had not been stripped of any power, that I was still a key figure in the team's future.

I didn't want to walk out at such a dark time in Dodger history. I didn't want to turn my back on the team I had been so instrumental in building throughout the previous dozen years.

So, I agreed to stay and see if I could repair the damage. But damage control was no easy task.

With losses in San Diego in the first two games of the trip, and another in the three previous games at Coors, the Dodgers stood at 36-37 starting play on that Sunday in late June, which left the club in third place, $11^1/2$ games out.

The continuing instability on the field wasn't my only concern on that trip to Denver.

On Friday night, as we were beating the Rockies, 4-3 in 10 innings, our publicity director, Derrick Hall, told me there was a story by *Baseball Weekly* writer Bob Nightengale circulating in the press box that claimed Whitey Herzog was to be named Dodger manager on Monday, replacing Bill Russell.

Normally, I could dismiss a report like that in a minute. But it was Nightengale who had broken the story earlier in the season of trade talk between the Dodgers and the Seattle Mariners involving their ace lefthander, Randy Johnson. That was interesting, since the only Dodger official who had any advance knowledge of that potential deal was Graziano.

Did Nightengale have a pipeline to Graziano? And was it possible that pipeline was again flowing with accurate information?

It was hard to believe the position I suddenly found myself in after three decades of being on top of everything Dodger related. Here I was, unable to comfortably dismiss a story having to do with a possible change in Dodger managers.

I tried to reach Graziano during that Friday night game, but was unsuccessful.

At that point, my gut reaction was to simply say the story wasn't true. If it turned out to indeed be true, it would be the last time I would tolerate a key Dodger personnel move coming my way from an outside party.

As it turned out, the Nightengale story was apparently a rehash of something he had written in *Baseball Weekly* the week before.

On Saturday, there was more unsettling news, and this time, there was no questioning its accuracy.

Talking by phone to our farm director, Charlie Blaney, I learned that Graziano had inquired about the weekend schedule of Glenn Hoffman, manager of our Triple A team in Albuquerque. Perhaps Bob was planning a trip to see the Albuquerque team. If so, he hadn't told his general manager about it.

Bob finally returned the calls I had made to his home Friday night on Saturday, reaching me at my hotel in Denver.

With the team returning home after Sunday's game, Bob and I agreed to meet Monday to discuss Russell's status and also plans for the payroll. Earlier, Graziano and I had agreed to discuss Russell's status at the All-Star break coming up in a few weeks. Graziano's time-table had obviously changed. I felt our sense of direction related to the payroll needed to be defined.

If there was another item to be added to the agenda, Bob didn't tell me on that Saturday.

On Sunday, with righthander Chan Ho Park on the mound for the finale of the series, we were struggling again, but it was hard for me to keep my mind on the game.

The day had begun pleasantly enough with a call to my daughter Jennifer at her Claremont apartment to wish her a happy 35th birthday. She used the occasion to wish me a happy Father's Day.

But the happiness soon faded.

The next call came from Eric Tracy, a Los Angeles radio reporter for KFWB.

"Al Campanis passed away last night," he told me, having learned the sad news from one of Al's neighbors, who also worked for KFWB.

The news was just about to break, and Eric wanted to know if he could get my response on tape. We made arrangements for Eric to call me back a little later.

When he did, I told Eric, as I told others that day, that Al Campanis, who had risen from player to general manager in the Dodger organization, was a man who devoted his life to his family and to baseball. His dedication to both knew no bounds. I had always respected Al as a baseball man, valued him as a friend and treasured the support he had shown me.

Al told me on a number of occasions that, when the Dodgers were discussing the idea of hiring me in 1969, he had enthusiastically endorsed me.

My life was inextricably tied to his. I had become the Dodger general manager only because of Al's unfortunate remarks on *Nightline* in 1987 that had cost him his job.

But beyond personal considerations, I felt the loss of one of the steadiest and oldest links to the Brooklyn years. I thought of this tragic news as the passing of an era.

How ironic considering that my own era would pass as well in just a few hours.

I first became concerned about my own fate in the eighth inning of a game we would go on to lose 11-6. Derrick Hall entered my box to inform me Graziano wanted me to call him at home.

With this being the finale of the series, I would be accompanying the team home that night. Bob asked if I could make a detour upon landing and come to Dodger Stadium for a meeting with him and Peter O'Malley before heading for my house. Bob also asked about Russell's schedule. I told Bob I assumed Bill would be heading to his Glendale home once we arrived at LAX.

A Sunday night meeting after a week away sounded awfully important, but I didn't push for details.

Still, I couldn't quite get it out of my mind. The team was struggling, the media was questioning the team's direction under the ownership of Rupert Murdoch's Fox Group and the fans were restless and unhappy after the Piazza trade.

So it might be time to designate a scapegoat.

Or two.

Had they decided to fire manager Bill Russell?

Or had they decided to fire both Russell *and* the general manager?

The normal postgame routine—the clubhouse meal, the showers, the sprint through autograph seekers to the bus, the banter on the way to the airport, the flight home to the accompaniment of shuffling cards—was all so familiar to me. I had been through it on hundreds of trips before, trips highlighted by noisy celebrations after big victories or deadened by the pall of devastating defeats. But this time, it all seemed to drag on so agonizingly.

When we landed, I and my wife, Sheryl, who had accompanied me on the trip, got into the sedan of Stan Kilpatrick, a driver who had driven us to and from the airport for years and had become a loyal friend in the process. On happier trips, there had been many pleasant conversations with Stan, but, on this night, it was quiet and tense as we drove.

When we pulled into parking lot 5 at the stadium, I got out and asked Stan to take Sheryl on to our home in Pasadena. A few scattered lights bathed the empty field in a beautiful glow. But the lights were on in many of the offices, a rare occurrence on a Sunday night with the team having been away.

I walked into Bob's office, but he said we would be meeting in Peter O'Malley's office. Peter was there awaiting us. There was little small talk about the team or the road trip. There obviously was a point to this meeting and Bob got right to it.

"We've decided to make a change in managers," he said, "and we are going to replace Bill Russell with Glenn Hoffman."

Then the other shoe hit the floor with a thud that shook my very being.

"Also, Fred," Bob continued, "I can't recommend you on a go-forward basis at the end of the season, and thus, I've decided to make Tommy Lasorda the interim general manager. Tommy will help us locate a permanent general manager."

At the age of 62, after a lifetime of steady employment in an unsteady field, I had just been fired for the first time. That I had lasted so long didn't lessen the blow, ease the pain or soften my resolve to maintain my dignity and my convictions.

Especially when Bob followed up his bombshell with a truly bizarre offer.

"We will pay off your contract," he said, "but if you would like to stay during a period of transition to assist Tommy, we would welcome that."

"If I stay for this period of transition," I asked Bob, "will I be compensated for it?"

"Oh no," he said, "you won't be paid additionally."

"In other words," I said, having trouble grasping the logic here, "I can come to work tomorrow, or Sheryl and I can go play golf tomorrow and I will be paid the same amount either way. Is that correct?"

"Correct."

"Bob, the only thing I really need to know," I said, the shock turning to anger, "is when I'll have a chance to clean out my office."

Mixed in with the anger was amazement that Peter had been present for the meeting. And that it had taken place in Peter's office. I had advised Peter for 30 years. If I had been asked about this meeting in advance—obviously I wasn't going to be—I would have told Peter not to get involved. I felt this was totally a Graziano-Fox move, not one where Peter should be present.

But, for one of the few times in three decades, Peter had not sought my advice.

I turned, went into my office and immediately called Sheryl.

"Are you sitting down?" I asked her.

"Why?" she said.

"I've just been fired. Would you come to Dodger Stadium and pick me up. We're going home."

"I'll be right there, Sweets," Sheryl replied.

Somehow, with her words, I knew there would be life after the Dodgers.

I left word with the guard at the Elysian Park entrance to ring me when Sheryl came through so she wouldn't have to come into the office. When the call came, I walked out through the glass doors at the entrance to the offices into a scene I'll never forget. At the top of the ramp leading to the parking lot was Sheryl's jeep. At the bottom was Bill Russell's car. He and his wife, Susan, had just pulled up in response to the call he had gotten at home from Graziano a half hour earlier.

Sheryl and I paused to embrace and then we walked down to the Russells. I told Bill I had just been fired and that Tommy was my replacement.

"They fired you?" Bill repeated, shock on his face as the words sunk in.

It all seemed so unreal, Bill and I with 60 years of Dodger blue between us, standing in the deserted Dodger Stadium parking lot on

*Fred with (from left to right) Bill Russell, Commissioner
Bowie Kuhn and Dodger Ted Sizemore at Dodgertown.*

our last night in the organization, the lights from our cars reflecting
off the trees and hills to provide the only illumination on this dark
moment in our lives.

"What about me?" asked Bill, pessimism in his voice.

"In all fairness," I said, knowing full well there was no fairness
in this whole deal, "I think it's better if Bob and Peter tell you what's
happening."

Bill didn't have to be told.

As he looked around in the darkness, as if in search of a ray of
hope, Bill spotted Tommy's car.

"I'm not going in that office if *he's* here," Bill said firmly.

At that moment, Derrick Hall came out looking for Bill. I asked Derrick to please make sure Tommy wasn't in Peter's office.

I didn't think he would be, but, on this night, there were no sure bets.

"I'm proud to have worked with you for 30 years," I told Bill. "You don't deserve what is happening."

Dodger Stadium had long seemed like home to me, but, deep down, I always knew there is a difference between where you work and where you live. It's just that the lines get blurred at times when you devote most of your life to a job.

I got into the passenger side of Sheryl's jeep and she got behind the wheel and began making the drive down from Dodger Stadium to the freeway below, a short drive I had made thousands of times in the previous 30 years.

I didn't look back, instead staring straight ahead as I realized I would never again have the same warm feeling about that drive.

CHAPTER II

THE BEGINNING

No matter how high we set our sights in life, it is clear to me the distance we travel is largely determined by the foundation from which we left.

I had a firm foundation, consisting of caring parents, Marston and Mary Frances, a brother, Doug, a sister, Lynn, and a wonderful childhood in Jamestown, Ohio.

My mother had been born in Jamestown where her father owned and operated a drugstore. A fire destroyed that store, but, years later, my father opened up his own drugstore right across the street from where the flames had engulfed his father-in-law's livelihood on the main business corner in town. We lived, for a while, in an apartment above my father's store.

For me, life in Jamestown was idyllic. I had my family, my friends, various school and sports activities, summer vacations at Indian Lake and several memorable fishing outings to Canada. I even experienced my first business ventures. My brother and I trapped muskrats (I still have one of the tags we used on our traps—CLAIRE BROTHERS, BOX 93, JAMESTOWN, OHIO) and I had a newspaper route, delivering the *Xenia Gazette*.

It's hard to know where the passion for a sport begins, but, for me and baseball, it probably was on those summer mornings when friends would come by and toss pebbles against the second-floor win-

*Fred with his mother, Mary Frances, and longtime friend Stan Kilpatrick
at a press conference in Pasadena, Calif., after Fred's firing by the Dodgers.*

dow of the bedroom I shared with Doug. It was the signal to get up,
get the baseball equipment and get moving to the diamond at a nearby
Silvercreek school.

Our friends came by not only out of friendship, but necessity as
well. My father sold a little baseball equipment at his all-purpose store,
which meant Doug and I controlled most of the bats and balls, and
the catcher's mask, for our games. So if there was to be a baseball

game in the neighborhood, chances were the Claire boys would be a part of it.

My love for baseball gradually became a burning fire. The fire was fueled by listening to the games from Crosley Field that were broadcast by Waite Hoyt ("Baumholtz goes up the terrace in left field to make the catch…") and by falling asleep on a Friday night with a radio in my ear, sending me the sounds of Bill Stern's sports show. I can remember wondering what would happen to me when I no longer had baseball as a passion in my life.

On one of those fishing trips, while walking along a lake, I spotted a faded newspaper left on the shore. Picking it up, I learned of the death of Babe Ruth from cancer.

That headline, that story, that wrinkled picture of The Babe became implanted in my mind, leaving an impression I carried into adulthood when, at first newspapers and then baseball, became my life.

I clearly remember the vending machines at Indian Lake into which you could put a nickel and receive a 3 x 5 card of a major leaguer, a Gus Zernial or a Red Schoendienst. I treated those cards as if they were $100 bills.

As my love of baseball continued to grow, the focus of my childhood shifted from Jamestown and Indian Lake and the fish pulled from Canadian waters to the lush grass, bright lights and the unforgettable excitement of Crosley Field.

It is 64 miles from Jamestown to Cincinnati, but for me, it might as well have been a journey to another world, the world of big-league baseball. Those family outings to Cincinnati to see the Reds at Crosley were magical trips for me.

I still have snapshots of those times. When I look at them, all the sounds and smells of Crosley are relived in my mind. It is again a summer day in 1948 and I'm watching major league baseball for the first time in the company of my family.

My brother Doug, a year and a half older than I, was a huge fan of Stan Musial and the St. Louis Cardinals. I'm not certain what inspired that. Perhaps it was the picture of Stan the Man on the Wheaties box.

In any case, Doug began to keep a scrapbook of the Cardinals during that 1948 season, clipping out the game stories from one of the newspapers sold at my father's drugstore and pasting them in a three-ring notebook.

You know how little brothers follow big brothers. So while Doug had the Cardinals to brag about, I rooted for the Reds.

Those family trips to Crosley, it seemed, always coincided with a visit by the Cardinals. Needless to say, the cheering from the Claire section tended to get a little heated.

My brother would root for Musial, Enos "Country" Slaughter, Red Schoendienst, Marty Marion, Whitey Kurowski, Del Rice, Chuck Diering, Howie Pollet, George "Red" Munger and Harry "The Cat" Brecheen.

My guys were Ray Lamanno, Ted Kluszewski, Bobby Adams, Virgil Stallcup, Grady Hatton, Hank Sauer, Johnny Wyrostek, Frankie Baumholtz, Bucky Walters, Ewell "The Whip" Blackwell and Herman Wehmeier.

I'll never forget the morning I awoke to find a *Cincinnati Enquirer* propped up on a chair beside my bed, placed there by my father.

To this day, I can still see the headline: "REDS TRADE SAUER AND BAUMHOLTZ FOR LOWREY AND WALKER." The Reds had traded Sauer, my favorite slugger, and Baumholtz to the Chicago Cubs for "Peanuts" Lowry and Harry "The Hat" Walker.

How could they make such a bad trade? I couldn't believe what I was reading.

I couldn't even imagine that someday I would be writing such headlines. And then, even more incredibly, later in life, I'd be making such headlines with trades of my own.

Back then, it would have been exciting enough for me to know that I would actually meet Sauer one day. I was with the Dodgers and Hank was a scout for the San Francisco Giants. I'll never forget shaking hands with him for the first time, gripping that huge right hand which I had seen so many times gripping a Louisville Slugger as if the bat had been placed in a vice.

Yet for all my fascination with baseball as a spectator sport, it was basketball I most enjoyed as a participant. I wanted more than anything to play on the varsity of the high school team, the Silvercreek Vikings. Nothing is bigger in those small Ohio towns than basketball.

But my dreams were not to be realized. In the summer of 1950, following my freshman year, my family and I moved to Southern California.

My ties to the past, though, would always endure.

In 1987, while on a road trip to Cincinnati with the Dodgers, I took my wife, Sheryl, to visit Jamestown. When we arrived, I parked the car near my father's old drugstore, by then an insurance office.

Across the street, a man was sitting in a swing on his front porch.

"Excuse me," I said, approaching him, "but do you know the Claire family?"

The gentleman thought a minute and then replied with a nod of his head, "Sure, Marston Claire owned the drugstore there on the corner. He and Mary Frances had three children and they used to live above the store."

It had been nearly 40 years since my family had left Jamestown, but we still had a place there in the minds of our old neighbors and friends.

Still, with my family's move, my future lay in Southern California. My father, having visited two brothers in Southern California, was enamored with the area. Blessed with an adventurous spirit, he gave up the store and our secure life in Jamestown and moved us west, where he opened a sundry store, complete with a pharmacy and fountain, in Redondo Beach.

Thank goodness for sports, because it eased the transition. Making new friends in high school can be difficult enough. Making new friends for a kid from Jamestown, who finds himself catapulted from the comfort of small-town America into the intimidating megalopolis of Southern California, can be traumatic.

But I found acceptance from my teammates in my new home in the South Bay when I joined the Torrance High basketball team.

I played baseball as well, but never got above the junior-varsity level in either sport.

No matter. My early love of baseball stayed with me, although now, instead of concentrating on the big leagues in general and Crosley Field in particular, I became a fan of the teams nearest to my new neighborhood. And in Los Angeles in the 1950s, that meant the L.A. Angels and Hollywood Stars of the Pacific Coast League. In that you pulled for either the Angels *or* the Stars, my team became the Stars.

Many of the Hollywood Stars of that period were men I would come to know personally later on in life, men like Monty Basgall, Chuck Stevens, Johnny O'Neil, George Genovese, Gail Henley, Ben Wade, Tommy Saffell and Bobby Bragan. During my years with the Dodgers, Basgall was a Dodger scout, minor league manager and coach. O'Neil, Genovese and Henley were scouts for the Dodgers in a department headed by Wade.

The Angels may have been the archrival of the Stars, but that didn't stop me from admiring two of their players who later became friends, two men I respected a great deal—Chuck Connors and Gene

Mauch. The Angels also had a lefthanded pitcher who later was to have an important role in my life—a fellow named Tommy Lasorda.

My other big interest in those days was journalism, and for that I can thank Myron Roberts. A teacher at Torrance High who added the management of the student newspaper to his duties, Roberts became a major influence in my life.

He certainly proved to be a major figure for me the day Ivan Malm, the Torrance vice principal, caught me playing basketball when I was supposed to be in class. Malm marched me directly over to Roberts' office. If Roberts hadn't been lenient with me, my dreams of a journalistic career might have ended right there.

It's amazing how much influence someone can have in your formative years. One high school teacher who cares can make a huge difference.

I was just as fortunate, in terms of a wonderful journalism instructor, when I entered El Camino College in the fall of 1953. W. A. (Bill) Kamrath, director of the journalism department, became my new guiding light.

Kamrath had a feature-writing class that culminated with each student submitting a story to several magazines with the hope of having it published. And just submitting the story wasn't enough. Along with creative writing, perseverance was required. A student needed three rejection slips to pass the class.

Either that, or a published story.

Deciding to concentrate on my chief outside interest, I wrote a piece entitled, "Make Way for the Coast League." The premise was that the Pacific Coast League (PCL), including teams from L.A., San Diego, San Francisco, Seattle and Oakland, could become a third major league.

I sent my story for consideration to several magazines and got two rejection slips in return. But, as the semester ended, I still hadn't received that third rejection, even though I had mailed a third copy of my story to *Baseball Magazine*.

I assured Kamrath I had complied with his rules, pleading for a better grade, but he wouldn't hear of it. With only two rejection slips in hand, he gave me a big, fat "C."

Several weeks after school had ended, I received a letter from *Baseball Magazine*. *Now* my rejection slip comes, I thought.

Wrong.

Inside the envelope, along with a letter, was a check. My article was going to be published.

I headed straight for school and proudly dropped that check on Kamrath's desk. My "C" instantly became an "A."

Five years before the Dodgers came West, I, at the age of 18, had an article in a baseball magazine theorizing that Los Angeles could support major-league baseball.

Years later, when I was a Dodger employee, I showed that article to owner Walter O'Malley with the same pride I had shown Kamrath my check, and O'Malley seemed just as impressed as Kamrath had been.

After a year at El Camino, another at Mt. San Antonio College and two at San Jose State, I had a bachelor's degree in journalism.

That *Baseball Magazine* article had given me confidence and my collegiate training had given me the tools to be a journalist, and I couldn't wait to make the big leap into the professional world.

No laying around all summer, enjoying a last hurrah, for me. That wasn't my style.

I graduated on a Sunday and had three job interviews lined up for Monday with newspapers in Pomona, Fullerton and Whittier.

The first was at 9 a.m. with Ted Johnson, managing editor of the *Pomona Progress-Bulletin*. First day, first interview and I already had a job offer.

Sort of.

Johnson told me that, if I could wait two weeks, he thought the City Hall beat would open up.

Thanks, but no thanks, I told him. Being young and bursting with enthusiasm, I couldn't wait that long to start to work.

My next stop was Fullerton where I learned the managing editor had left early for a luncheon meeting. His secretary assured me her boss would see me as soon as he finished the two-hour meeting.

Thanks, but no thanks, I told her, but I couldn't wait two hours because I was on a fast track to find a job.

Quite honestly, to this day, I can't explain what motivated me, fresh out of college with only part-time experience working professionally in the newspaper business, to be so impatient and so cavalier with journalistic opportunities. All I knew was that I wanted and needed a job, and I was supremely confident about my chances of finding one.

And sure enough, at the third interview, I got my job.

In the early afternoon, I met with Mel Rich, managing editor of the *Whittier Daily News*. He wasn't out to lunch. And he didn't tell me to wait two weeks. He had a position right now, in the sports department of all places, and it was mine for the taking at $65 a week.

I took it.

After working there for a year, I left to serve a six-month stint in the Army Reserve. While on duty, I learned there had been a fire at the Whittier paper, causing major damage.

Did I still have a job? I asked that question of Rich via a letter. Yes I did, he wrote me back. Not only that, but a better job than the one I had left. When I returned, I would be sports editor.

Great news? Not really, because the sports editor at the time, Willie Mears, was a friend of mine and had a wife and a child. I couldn't take his job. We remain friends to this day.

So when I returned from active duty, instead of going to Whittier, I went back to Pomona to see Johnson, and this time he hired me right away. And this time, it was for his sports department.

I have wonderful memories of my time with the *Progress-Bulletin*. The paper was owned and operated by the Richardson family—A.T. and his son Charles—and they had put together an experienced and talented editorial staff. Gene Earl was the sports editor when I joined the newspaper, and Jerry Miles had just been hired as a member of the sports department.

When the Dodgers came to L.A. in 1958, our paper, like most of the others in the area, gave the team huge coverage. One of my earliest thrills in sportswriting came the day before my 24th birthday. It was the end of the 1959 season and the Dodgers were in the World Series against the Chicago White Sox. The first two games were in Chicago, but when the clubs took the field at the L.A. Coliseum for Game 3 on October 4 in front of a World Series-record crowd of 92,294, I was there as a member of the working press. The Dodgers, behind starter Don Drysdale and reliever Larry Sherry, won 3-1. The next day, my game story appeared in the *Progress-Bulletin*, making it a very happy birthday indeed. It was the Dodgers' first World Series victory in Los Angeles, and I was on hand to see it and report on the game.

In the early 1960s, when Gene Earl left to go to the *L.A. Times*, I became the sports editor, achieving the position I had turned down in Whittier, and Jerry Miles became my assistant.

Even though I was in charge, I still managed to cover some Dodger games, including their appearances in the 1963 and '65 World Series.

We worked hard to build the *Progress-Bulletin* sports department into what generally was acknowledged as one of the finest suburban sports sections in Southern California and received validation for our efforts by winning several California Newspaper Publishers

Association awards. Gordon Verrell and Bill Langley had joined me and Jerry to complete our staff as the sports section expanded. Our success was based on a balancing act. We managed to cover the Dodgers and the other top professional teams in the area, while also giving full coverage to our local high schools and small colleges.

But this wonderful period in my life wasn't to last. In 1968, the Richardsons sold the paper to the DonRey Media Group. The family feeling followed them out the door. Suddenly, we were dealing with a large chain that wanted us to do more at less cost.

I could see it was time to move on.

In May of 1968, I learned through a friend (Bob Barker of the Garden Grove newspaper, a classmate at San Jose State) the Angel beat was opening up at the *Long Beach Independent Press-Telegram* because beat writer Ross Newhan had been hired by the *L.A. Times*.

Contacted about the job, I interviewed with John Dixon, the Long Beach sports editor. I thought the interview went well, but John didn't offer me the job.

Still, I felt I should let the *Progress-Bulletin* know what was going on. I went in to see Joe Gendron, who had replaced Ted Johnson as managing editor, and told Joe that, because of the cutbacks at the paper, I was thinking about moving on.

His reaction was to wish me luck, if I made the move.

Obviously, they weren't going to go overboard to keep me, and Joe acknowledged that the new ownership group was going to make significant changes in the way we covered the news. Mentally, I was out the door before my meeting with Gendron had even ended.

There was only one problem: I had no place to go.

I called Dixon back and told him I had to know if his newspaper had a serious interest in hiring me.

Yes, he said, the job of Angel beat writer was mine if I wanted it. Boy, did I want it.

I began covering the Angels on Memorial Day, 1968. I found myself surrounded by wonderful people, starting with the manager, Bill Rigney, pitching coach Bob Lemon and players like Jim Fregosi, Buck Rodgers and Bobby Knoop.

When I introduced myself to Rodgers, I explained that I was coming from the Pomona paper.

"Everyone has to start someplace," he said with a smile.

Those words always stuck with me, as did my warm feelings for Rodgers.

I only stayed with the Angels for the remainder of that 1968 season. With a wife and three young children, I found the travel and my time away from home difficult. I understood that a player or club official had to make that kind of sacrifice in lifestyle, but I felt a writer had other options.

What those options were, however, I wasn't sure.

Had I made a mistake in leaving the *Progress-Bulletin* where I enjoyed the responsibility of being a sports editor, and had freedom in writing a column and covering events of my choice? All of that and minimal travel and time away from home. I did my best to shake these thoughts. I wasn't going back now.

Uncertain of where I was going, however, I suddenly found an open door before me. The highly respected George Lederer, who had covered the Dodgers for the *Press-Telegram* since the team's arrival 11 seasons earlier, was leaving to become public relations director for the Angels.

John Dixon asked me if I wanted the Dodger beat. But there was a condition attached. He wanted me to commit to that beat for at least two seasons. Finding writers willing to endure the grind of spring training and the 162 games that follow, to live out of a suitcase for up to nine months, to often put their lives and their families on hold, had become tougher and tougher. John wanted to know that he was at least set for the near future on what he considered one of the most important beats on the newspaper.

So here I was, having questioned my desire to cover baseball after little more than half a season with the Angels, now being asked to sign up for two years with the Dodgers.

Despite my concerns, I told John I would do it. I felt the opportunity to be involved with the historic Dodger franchise was too great to turn down.

My introduction to the team came in 1969 at the club's spring training complex, known as Dodgertown, located on the east coast of Florida.

The facility had been a naval air station until the end of World War II when the government turned it over to the city of Vero Beach. A Vero Beach businessman, Bud Holman, made the match between the facility, in need of a tenant, and the Dodgers, in need of a permanent spring training site.

Dodgertown—a navy barracks transformed into dorms that were eventually replaced with a 90-room housing facility, an on-site stadium, numerous other diamonds, additional mounds and batting cages and sliding pits, a media workroom and photo darkroom, a medical department, trainers' rooms, dining rooms, a broadcast center, a picturesque golf course, a lounge area complete with poker and pool tables, along with a swimming pool and tennis and basketball courts and other recreational facilities—soon became the blueprint for so many other major-league organizations.

Upon my arrival, I quickly learned this was not only a special facility, but it was run by a special organization with very special people. And it all started with Walter and Kay O'Malley and the tone they set.

Walter was always buzzing from one point to another in his golf cart, or seated in the middle of the action, running the nightly poker game in the lounge.

He didn't just use that cart for Dodger matters. He and Kay would spend their days swinging their clubs on the course.

Before Walter would excuse himself in the evening to the delights of the green-felt table and the stacks of poker chips, he and Kay would host the extended Dodger family in the lounge. Vice-president Al Campanis and his wife, Bess, would be there as would be coaches Red Adams and his wife, Betty, Monty Basgall and his wife, Nita, manager Walt Alston and his wife, Lela, the Dodger front office staff, including public relations vice-president Red Patterson and his wife, Helen, along with various members of the media and friends of the O'Malley family.

But the O'Malleys didn't just entertain the big shots. Everyone from the secretaries to the clubhouse people could also be found in that lounge enjoying the O'Malley's hospitality.

With Walter O'Malley around, there was plenty of good-natured fun. When the wheels to his golf cart disappeared one spring, a major investigation ensued. The pilfered wheels were finally discovered in Tommy Lasorda's room, but it ultimately turned out that the prankster had been Jimmy Lefebvre.

There was a true Dodger spirit in the air that you couldn't help but feel and want to be a part of.

I got my chance to become part of it in June of 1969.

Red Patterson's famous temper had flared one evening at his assistant, Howard Handy, and word quickly spread that a search was underway for Handy's replacement.

I saw my way out of baseball beat writing. About to leave on an East Coast trip with the Dodgers, I paused to write Red a letter, telling him I was interested in the job.

Arthur (Red) Patterson shows a young Fred the ropes in 1969.

I didn't see or hear from Red until the end of the trip, which concluded in San Diego. It was there that he informed me he had decided to offer the position to Don Andersen, sports information director at USC. Andersen had been very successful in a very short space of time at USC, earning the respect of the local media.

I told Red he had made a good choice and wished him and Andersen well.

End of story?

Hardly. Andersen ultimately turned the job down when USC made a strong push, including more money, to keep him. Don told me recently that he felt if he left his job with the Trojans after only a couple of years, it wouldn't be fair and it wouldn't look good on his resume. When the road trip ended, Red asked me to go to lunch with him at one of his favorite Glendale restaurants, the Thistle Inn. Red gave me the good news before lunch was even served. That was Red's way, right to the point. Red said he had met with the O'Malleys, Walter and Peter, and they had decided to offer me the job.

I smiled and shook my head. Sorry, I said, I wasn't interested, clearly shocking Red.

"But," said Red, "I thought this is what you wanted."

It had been, but since the Dodgers hadn't made me their first choice, I told him, it indicated to me they didn't have confidence in my ability to fill the position. So, I was content to remain a beat writer.

But Red was persistent. Once it had been decided the Dodger officials wanted me, he was determined to get me. There were more meetings and more luncheons.

The decision to move from writing to public relations was a move I thought about a great deal. Did I really want to give up reporting for what I saw initially as a service type of position?

One of my best friends at the time (and he still is today, I'm happy to say) was John Wiebusch, who had covered the Angels in 1968 and was covering the Dodgers in 1969 for the *Los Angeles Times*.

"Fred, you don't want to go into PR," he told me. "You can write and you should be a writer. PR is no place for you."

John said he would do his best to see if there might be an opportunity for me to join the *Los Angeles Times*.

I gave John's comments a lot of thought, but I wanted to do less traveling and, in the end, I took the job with the Dodgers on July 14, 1969.

That very day, I received a call from Marshall Klein, sports editor of the *L.A. Times* Orange County edition. Marshall offered me a job.

"Marshall, why couldn't you have called a day ago or two days ago?" I responded. "I can't go down the hall and tell Peter O'Malley I'm leaving on my first day on the job."

One day can indeed change a lifetime.

One of my first duties was a road trip to San Francisco. The day the trip ended and I returned to my Pomona home was July 20—the day Neil Armstrong walked on the moon. The world and my small universe had changed forever.

I hadn't informed John Dixon of the change in my life until the end because I had firmly believed, despite my talks with Red, that I was going to stay with the *Press-Telegram*.

It was only after I finally accepted the Dodger offer that I made the call.

"John," I said, "I told you I would stay with the Dodgers for two years if I took the beat. I'm going to stay with the Dodgers, John, but I'm afraid my position has changed."

I, of course, stayed with the Dodgers for 30 years and I'm confident John believes I fulfilled my end of the deal.

CHAPTER III

BLUE HEAVEN

In July of 1969, I was just a young guy of 33 with no gray in my hair and plenty of energy in my body.

Here I was, publicity director of the Dodgers and surrounded by some of the great people in the game—Walter Francis O'Malley, the man who had opened up the western half of the country to the big leagues by moving the Dodgers from Brooklyn, Walter Alston, a legendary manager from a small Ohio town, and senior Dodger executives such as Al Campanis, Bill Schweppe and Red Patterson.

My timing couldn't have been better from the standpoint of the makeup of the front office, and the talent that had been injected into the organization as a result of the June draft of 1968, players such as infielders Steve Garvey, Ron Cey, Davey Lopes and Bobby Valentine, outfielders Bill Buckner and Tom Paciorek, catcher Joe Ferguson and pitchers Doyle Alexander, Geoff Zahn and Sandy Vance.

It was an organization about to undergo a remarkable transition, and I was going to be along for the ride of my life.

At the start of that 1969 season, Buzzie Bavasi, Dodger executive vice-president, the team's general manager for nearly two decades and the architect of the great Brooklyn teams of the '50s, had left to become president of an expansion team, the San Diego Padres. Walter used the occasion to elevate his son Peter, then in charge of stadium operations, to the post of executive vice-president. Campanis moved up from scouting director to vice-president for player personnel and scouting. Schweppe also reached the V.P. level as the man in charge of minor-league operations.

It was clear Peter was going to run the business side, with Campanis, Schweppe and Alston handling the baseball side. Red was my immediate boss as the V.P. in charge of public relations and promotions.

All of these men had served the Dodgers all the way back to the Brooklyn days, giving the club a solid foundation.

In the spring of 1970, Peter was elevated once again, this time to team president, with Walter O'Malley becoming chairman of the board. The title of executive vice-president would not be used again until a dozen years later when it would be given to me.

But such lofty thoughts were the last thing on my mind when I joined the organization. I was just trying to grasp the time and dedication required to function in this fascinating new world I had entered. I stepped on a treadmill the first day I took my place in the front office and had to quickly learn to keep pace.

My life was the Dodgers, 24 hours a day, seven days a week. I not only accepted that, but thrived on it.

The work ethic of the members of the front office was astounding. For game days at Dodger Stadium, we would arrive by 9 a.m. if not earlier, and stay until an hour or so after the game. Sometimes, that meant working until nearly midnight.

That was particularly true if you were working for and with Red Patterson, a man whose passion for his job was legendary. Red couldn't wait to get to work in the morning, and he never seemed in a hurry to go home.

Ten-game homestands and 15-hour days were the norm, and there was no such thing as a vacation.

When I first joined the Dodgers, three people—Red, myself and his secretary, Janet Calderwood—handled a vast array of duties including: publicity, public relations, promotions, publications, films, community relations, speakers' bureau, sponsorships, season and group sales, pregame activities, the message board (later becoming Diamond Vision), photography assignments, team statistics and fan mail.

Once the game started, Red and I would take our seats in the press box, Red in the first row, right next to public address announcer John Ramsey, and within a wave of the hand of both the message-board operator and Dodger Stadium organist Helen Dell. I would be seated in the second row, first seat to the left of the aisle where I could answer questions and satisfy requests of the surrounding media. There wasn't anything said over the PA or run on the message board that Red and I didn't know about.

For Red, it was heaven. He was right where he wanted to be, at the controls in the press box, the game on the field, his dinner in front of him and his traditional vodka martini by his side. He had earned that drink.

Red understood the transition I was making from writing to publicity. He had been a writer himself back in New York before making the switch to publicity when he joined the Yankees in the 1940s. Even in blasé New York, where they thought they had seen it all, Red made a name for himself by giving them something they *hadn't* seen: the tape-measure home run.

All the way back to the days of Babe Ruth, and maybe even before, broadcasters, reporters and fans loved to speculate about the length of home runs. They would chronicle the number of homers hit out of a park, or onto the roof, or into the upper deck.

Or they would simply spout out an alleged distance. *That ball traveled 480 feet. No, it was 502. Wrong, 506.*

Nobody really knew. This was, of course, before the speed gun and other electronic gear that today measures every aspect of the game scientifically. So Red came up with the idea of a tape measure.

He would make a big show of literally measuring the spot a ball had landed from home plate by tape measure and then publicizing that figure.

It began with a gargantuan home run hit by Mickey Mantle against lefthander Chuck Stobbs of the old Washington Senators at Griffith Stadium on April 17, 1953.

After Mantle's blow cleared a 55-foot wall in left field, Yankee announcer Mel Allen, after calling it one of the longest home runs he had ever seen, informed his listeners that "Yankee publicity director Red Patterson has gotten hold of a tape measure and he's going to go out there to see how far that ball actually did go."

The figure Patterson came up with was 565 feet.

Were Red's figures always accurate? Who knew? But of this there was no dispute: Red's tape-measure numbers became conversation pieces, causing everybody to talk about his hitters and his team.

Red, as always, had done his job.

To this day, long home runs are called tape-measure shots.

Red was also credited with starting Cap Day in New York.

In Los Angeles, Red saw himself as the shepherd of the Dodger beat writers. He loved coming up with bits of information and unusual statistics, tape-measure blasts being only the beginning. Red's favorite writer was Bob Hunter of the *Herald-Examiner*, the man nicknamed "Chopper" by Walter O'Malley because of the way he would divide up and arrange his chips in the Dodgertown poker games.

Bob and Red had a special affinity, because they were close in age, and Bob was the most experienced baseball writer in Los Angeles, having previously covered the Pacific Coast League.

In my first season, I had a special affinity for several players, one of them being second baseman Ted Sizemore.

Sizemore had started his career as a catcher, but he was small in stature. His attributes were quick hands and good hand-eye coordination, which made it logical to switch him to the infield.

He was a rookie in 1969, having a good season, and I was a rookie publicity director trying to have a good season. We clicked almost immediately and became good friends.

The players loved Red Patterson because they knew he knew the game, and because they knew he cared about them. He showed me that you connect by caring.

I worked hard to get Ted the national attention he deserved and, a couple of months after the season ended, I learned people had indeed been paying attention to his accomplishments. We were together on the golf course when the good news reached us: Ted Sizemore had been named National League Rookie of the Year.

I didn't just deal with rookies. Sometimes, I got to deal with legends. I will never forget June 4, 1972, the date Jackie Robinson, who broke big-league baseball's color barrier as a Dodger in 1947, made an appearance at Dodger Stadium for a long overdue moment, the retiring of his uniform.

As part of Oldtimers Day, three uniforms were retired, perhaps the three most noteworthy in Dodger history: Robinson's No. 42, Sandy Koufax's No. 32 and Roy Campanella's No. 39.

There's a picture from that event that best freezes the moment. Jackie is wearing a short-sleeved white shirt with blue pants and a blue tie. Campy, wheelchair bound since his 1958 auto accident, has on a Brooklyn cap and is wearing a Dodger jersey. And then there is Sandy in full uniform, looking every bit as though he could go out and start that day's game. The three men are holding large glass frames containing their legendary uniforms.

Fred (not in uniform) at a Dodger Fantasy Camp with Dodger greats (from left) Carl Furillo, Duke Snider, Carl Erskine, Roy Campanella, Ted Sizemore, Willie Davis and Don Drysdale.

What the picture doesn't show, however, is the commotion just before the start of the ceremonies.

Jackie was standing near the steps of the Dodger dugout when a fan in the seats directly above shouted, "Jackie, Jackie, please sign this ball."

The man tossed it in Jackie's direction, not realizing his vision had deteriorated so badly because of retinal bleeding that he had no way of seeing the ball.

It bounced off Jackie's shoulder and hit him in the head. The people around Jackie went wild with anger, shouting at the man who had made the ill-advised throw.

But above those loud voices came the soothing voice of Jackie Robinson.

"Give me the ball," he said. "Calm down and give me the ball. He doesn't know." Jackie borrowed a pen, signed the ball and had it returned to the fan.

While people around him were shouting and losing control, understandable as that was, Jackie retained his presence and responded with dignity. Upset as he may have been at being struck, he wasn't going to allow his emotions to dictate his response.

I never had the opportunity to see Jackie Robinson, the ballplayer, in person, but I had just witnessed the very essence of Jackie Robinson, the man.

Four months later, Robinson was at Riverfront Stadium in Cincinnati to throw out the first ball in the 75th World Series.

Before the ceremonies, I was standing in an area leading to the field with a small group, which included Jackie and Peter O'Malley, when we were approached by a man who Jackie, because of his failing eyesight, didn't recognize immediately.

"Jackie, it's Pee Wee," someone said as Robinson's old teammate, Pee Wee Reese, came closer. The two embraced.

As frail as he had become, Jackie went to that World Series game because he had a message he wanted to deliver.

"I'd like to see a black manager," he said over national television. "I'd like to see the day when there is a black man coaching third base."

Nine days after that appearance, on October 24, 1972, Jackie Robinson passed away at the age of 53.

Meeting Jackie and his wonderful wife, Rachel, was a career highlight for me.

There would certainly be several others as I became more and more involved in the operation of the team.

I was invited to attend meetings Peter held with the team vice-presidents. I always felt comfortable in that environment even though I was only a department head, not a V.P.

My comfort level came from the fact Peter had a lot of confidence in me. That eased me into expressing my views in those meetings, even though I might have an opinion that conflicted with one of the vice-presidents.

But as much as I enjoyed my position, I was tempted to leave in 1973. More than tempted, actually. I did leave for a blink of the eye.

My good friend John Wiebusch had asked me to join him in the National Football League Creative Services office run out of Los Angeles, and I had agreed.

But when I went to Peter with the news, he wasn't willing to let me go that easily. He told me he had been planning to put me in charge of the public relations and marketing departments, to replace Red, because Red was nearing retirement age.

I told Peter I didn't think that was fair to Red, and besides, the way Red worked, it would take more than one person to replace him.

But Peter didn't give up. He stayed on me day after day, even though I was already on lame-duck status.

And gradually, he began to get to me. It wasn't so much that Peter was offering me additional money to stay. It was his obvious sincerity in wanting me to remain, wanting me to be a key figure in the Dodgers' future.

Finally, I gave in. Now, I was faced with one of the hardest tasks of my career, telling John Wiebusch I wouldn't be joining him after all even though I had given my word. That was the worst part, something I have thought about many times over the years.

The easy part was telling Peter he had won me over.

"If you ever wanted to get rid of me, you've lost a great opportunity," I told him as we met at the entrance to the Dodger Stadium offices on the day I decided to turn my back on the NFL.

So I stayed, Red stayed and I continued learning my craft under him until it all came to a sudden end on a Friday in February of 1975. Red looked up at me in the office that day and asked me the directions to Lakeside Country Club.

A strange question, coming from Red.

"You've been to Lakeside a million times," I said. "You know the way."

"No, remind me how to get there," Red said again. "And I want to tell you something. If you have to reach me tomorrow, I won't be at home and I can't tell you where I'll be. Understand? It's very confidential."

This was getting stranger by the minute.

"Red," I said, "tomorrow is Saturday and I'm not going to need to reach you. Nothing is happening. I'm going to be playing golf at Los Serranos with [ticket manager] Walter Nash."

Red was never good at keeping secrets, but I wasn't very good at figuring this one out. He was trying to tell he would be at Lakeside Saturday for a very important meeting.

I didn't know much about Lakeside, but I might have put two and two together if I had remembered one of that club's members was a good friend of Red's—Angel owner Gene Autry.

As Nash and I came up the 18th fairway at Los Serranos, a man named Ells, an old friend from my Pomona newspaper days, popped out of the starter's shack located between the 18th green and the first tee and waved me down.

"Fred, you have a call here on this phone," he said, pointing to the shack.

This, of course, was before we all became reachable at all times through the advent of the cell phone.

With my ball already on the 18th green, I moved quickly over to the shack, somewhat stunned anybody could find me and concerned over what could be so important.

"Fred, this is Peter O'Malley," said the voice on the end, "Red Patterson has just resigned to become president of the Angels. I want to meet you tonight at the baseball writers' dinner at the Biltmore Hotel."

I returned to the green, prepared to putt, and then, before stroking the ball, looked up and said, "Walter, Red has just resigned."

As I looked out of the corner of my eye while pretending to line up the shot, I thought Walter Nash's ever-present cigar was about to drop out of his mouth.

That night, Peter pulled me aside before dinner at the Biltmore and, as always, got directly to the point.

"Fred," he said, "I have met with my dad and we agree you are the man to replace Red. We don't agree on the money. My dad only wants to raise you $1,500 a year."

"Peter," I replied, "I'm honored that you and your father believe I'm the man for the job. I'm not worried about the money. This is a very important job. If I do it well, I know you'll pay me what the job is worth. If I don't do the job well, do yourself a favor and fire me."

Peter smiled and stuck out his hand, saying, "You've got yourself a deal."

I was now vice-president of public relations and promotions for the Los Angeles Dodgers. With my new title came new responsibilities and new opportunities to make an impact on the organization.

I made an impact in 1977 when the Dodgers were looking for a third broadcaster to join Vin Scully and Jerry Doggett. I was interested in Ross Porter, who was then the sports anchor at KNBC, Channel 4.

But I have to admit I had a little fun with Ross. I asked him if he knew anybody who might be interested in the job.

He called me back instantly.

"Yeah, me," he said.

And he's been with the team ever since.

Another member of the Dodger broadcast crew is Rick Monday. Those who go back a couple of decades remember Rick not as a member of the team in the broadcast booth, but rather the team on the field. It was Rick's ninth-inning home run in the deciding game of the 1981 National League Championship Series against the Montreal Expos that gave our club a 2-1 victory and a World Series berth against the Yankees. We went on to beat the Yanks in six games.

Those with even longer memories, however, will remember another memorable Monday moment in the Dodger Stadium outfield.

And Rick wasn't even a Dodger at the time.

It was April 25, 1976. Rick was a Chicago Cub outfielder that Sunday afternoon, just taking his position as the Dodgers came to bat in the fourth inning.

At that moment, an unemployed spectator from Eldon, Mo., 37-year-old William Errol Thomas, and his young son ran onto the field with an American flag and a container of lighter fluid which Thomas proceeded to sprinkle on the flag in full view of the crowd of 25,167.

Others were frozen at the sight, but not Monday. He raced over and scooped up the flag, before it could be ignited, and carried it to safety.

National anthem singer Frank Sinatra
visits with Fred on opening day of 1977.

Sitting in the press box, I turned to our message-board opera-tor, Jeff Fellenzer, and told him to type the words: "Rick Monday.....You Made a Great Play."

At first, the crowd was stunned by the whole scene. But then, applause built slowly and steadily, until finally, the fans broke into a stirring rendition of "God Bless America."

I got a call in the press box from Walter O'Malley, who told me, "Fred, this will go down as one of the great moments in Dodger Sta-dium history."

He was right. *Herald-Examiner* photographer James Roark's photo of Monday saving the flag was nominated for a Pulitzer Prize.

In the ensuing years, the incident remains as fresh and inspirational in the minds of those who saw it as the day it happened.

A year later, the Dodgers traded outfielder Bill Buckner, infielder Ivan De Jesus and pitcher Jeff Albert to Chicago to acquire Monday, along with pitcher Mike Garman.

It was a homecoming for Monday, who had played at Santa Monica High School before going on to Arizona State and then becoming the first pick in the first amateur draft back in 1965.

So Monday came home as a Cub and saved a flag, then wound up back home as a Dodger and slugged a home run to win a flag.

My duties as a Dodger vice-president reached into many areas. In terms of marketing impact, nothing matched the publicity tool I helped to create prior to the 1977 season, a creation recognized throughout the baseball universe by two words: Dodger Blue.

I had always been impressed by the way the major colleges in this country have been able to develop a great spirit among their fans. From Notre Dame football to Indiana basketball, there was a special flavor to these programs. And a central component of that flavor were colors, from the gold of the Fighting Irish's helmets to the bright red of the Hoosiers' uniforms.

So why not add a color to the Dodger identification, Dodger Blue?

The start of the 1977 season seemed the perfect time to launch our new blue marketing view. We had a highly visible and energetic new manager in Tommy Lasorda. If we could mix the paint properly, I knew Tommy would be the perfect person to spread the blue all over town.

It ended up being spread all over the world.

At the time, we held a public workout every February at Dodger Stadium, which included an exhibition game against coach Rod Dedeaux's USC baseball team. With admission free, it wasn't unusual to have 30,000-plus fans show up. We would promote the workout like crazy, and then give the impression we were shocked that so many fans had been in attendance.

That 1977 workout was to feature the debut of the Dodger Blue campaign. Tommy had been alerted to the plan and would be talking Dodger Blue until he was blue in the face. Advertisements in the newspaper would encourage fans to wear blue to the game.

On the night before the workout, at a dinner which included Peter O'Malley, Nash, the ticket manager, Bob Smith, director of stadium operations, and me, Peter came up with the final touch. Home plate and the other bases would be painted blue for the occasion and a fresh coat of blue would be put on the outfield wall. Smith excused himself from the table, made a call and reached the man who handled all the painting at Dodger Stadium. The guy went to work that night.

And thus was born Dodger Blue.

If you look back to written or broadcast material Dodger related prior to 1977, you won't find particular mention of Dodger blue. But ever since then, there has been a steady stream of such references, from Think Blue to Dodger Blue Wrecking Crew.

But the best marketing campaign in the world doesn't work if you have nothing to sell. Nobody would get excited about the term Dodger Blue Wrecking Crew if we had a crew that wasn't capable of wrecking anything other than their own season.

Fortunately, we had talent worthy of the name through much of the 1970s. The most memorable group from the era was Garvey, Lopes, Russell and Cey. Even today, the names seem to come out together almost as if they were connected.

And they were as no other infield in history.

First baseman Steve Garvey, second baseman Davey Lopes, shortstop Bill Russell and third baseman Ron Cey started together for the first time as a unit on June 23, 1973, and stayed together for a record

Dodger first baseman Steve Garvey and Fred Claire.

eight and a half seasons, including four pennants and one world championship.

The four were alike in many ways on the field. All four were great competitors who played through pain and injury. All four were remarkable athletes who were standouts in several sports in high school.

Russell and Lopes both started in the Dodger organization as outfielders, but were moved to the middle of the infield to take advantage of their speed and great hand-eye coordination.

It was Russell who came first, making the team in the spring of 1969. Walt Alston liked the young kid with the appealing personality, a small-town guy like himself. For Walt, it was Darrtown, Ohio, for Russell, Pittsburg, Kansas.

Russell had speed to burn and displayed the attitude that he would do whatever it took to make the team and please the manager.

He had spent the 1968 season, his third in the minors, at Bakersfield as an outfielder. He was only 20 years old, but Walt wasn't checking IDs. And he didn't need a stopwatch to tell him the kid could fly. Walt wanted Russell on the big club the next season, and Walt got his way.

It wasn't until 1973 that the other three forced their way into the starting lineup.

Garvey had started out as a third baseman, but his muscular upper body made his throws an endless adventure. However, he had good hands, proving to be a sure-handed first baseman who was excellent at scooping bad throws out of the dirt.

Cey had limited range as a third baseman, but he picked up everything within his reach. Once he got his glove on the ball, the runner could figure he was on borrowed time.

Lopes didn't arrive in Los Angeles with much fanfare, and that was just the way he liked it. I recall that, while I was driving Davey to a sportscasters' luncheon, he confided in me that, "I'm glad I don't have all of the attention of Garvey or the others. They can have it."

But in time, Lopes was to prove himself deserving of some of that attention as he established himself as one of the great clutch performers in the game.

The arrival of Garvey, Cey and Lopes in the 1973 season coincided with the addition of Lasorda and Monty Basgall to Alston's coaching staff. That was a great move by general manager Al Campanis. Garvey, Cey and Lopes had played under Tommy. Basgall was simply the best infield instructor I have ever known, and you could get a lot of baseball people to second that opinion. It was Monty who took the lead in helping Russell and Lopes make the transition from the outfield. It was Monty who played a key role in Garvey's move from third.

But while Garvey and Cey may have had great cohesion at the corners of the infield, they were just as far removed off the field. They never seemed to connect except on infield grounders.

For all four of those players, as a matter of fact, the similarities were confined to the playing field. I certainly wouldn't describe the group as one big, happy family.

Russell's easygoing nature and quick wit enabled him to get along with and poke fun at everyone, but when it came to Garvey, there was definitely a distance between him and his fellow infielders.

From the start, Steve was very conscious of his image and his place in the community. As someone involved in the marketing and PR efforts of the Dodgers at that time, I thought it was great for the team. It was just Steve being Steve, his true nature. He was friendly, always reaching out to the fans, always polite and cooperative with the press, good days or bad.

As a result, Steve gained a lot of attention in the media. It was something he sought and something I thought he deserved.

But my feeling is that it didn't always play well with Davey and Ron. They, too, were cooperative with the media, but I don't think they really cared whether the attention came their way or not.

And it wasn't just Davey and Ron who felt Steve got too cozy with the media at times. There was a famous clubhouse wrestling and shoving match between Steve and Don Sutton in 1977 in New York. The confrontation became headlines for a day, but it didn't really amount to much in the long run.

For all the differences that may have existed, the competitive drive of those players is the thing I will always remember.

In my mind, it's summarized by a scene in the dugout before a postseason game in the late 1970s. It was a season when, it seemed to me, Steve and Ron hadn't spoken more than 10 words to one another.

On that day, Ron was not in the lineup, sidelined by a wrist injury.

I was in the dugout as Steve walked up the runway and went to the rack to check his bats. Ron came up, gave him a pat on the back and said in a low voice, "Go get 'em, Garv."

Steve turned around and replied, "Thanks, Ronnie."

Not a long conversation, but long enough to tell you all you really need to know about the overwhelming competitive drive they possessed. Whatever their differences, those four will forever be linked in history. I'm happy their ultimate image will be four young men, standing shoulder to shoulder, wearing the Dodger uniform and giving the appearance they were brothers.

CHAPTER IV

WALT AND WALTER

They had the same first name. At different levels in different capacities, they both ran the Dodgers. But there, the similarities ended. Walt Alston and Walter O'Malley were as different as could be, in background and personality. Nevertheless, my relationship with each was just as solid in its own unique way. It would be impossible for me to recall my years with the Dodgers without singling out these two people who fall into a very special category.

THE FIELD BOSS

Walt had been the Dodger manager for 15 years when I joined the team in 1969, and we were separated in age by 24 years, but, regardless of that, we forged an instant and lasting bond because of our upbringing, both of us having been raised in small Ohio towns.

Although he traveled all over the world and managed in both Brooklyn and Los Angeles, Darrtown, Ohio remained the only permanent home Walt ever had.

Or ever wanted.

Fred with former Dodger manager Leo Durocher,
Al Campanis and pitcher Pete Richert (from left) .
Leo served on Walt Alston's coaching staff.

I used to kid him that, compared to Darrtown, my hometown
of Jamestown (population 1,500), was a metropolis. Walt's grand-
daughter, Kim Ogle, once told me the population of Darrtown was
500, but admitted, "That may have included the family pets."

A career minor leaguer with one major league at-bat—he struck
out—Alston was a surprise choice to manage the Brooklyn Dodgers
in 1954. It was a high-profile team that drew national interest despite

playing in the shadow of the New York Yankees. It was the team that had broken the color barrier in 1947 with Jackie Robinson. It was the team of Pee Wee and the Duke, Campy and Hodges, Oisk and Skoonj (To those unfamiliar with the Bums of Brooklyn, that's Pee Wee Reese, Duke Snider, Roy Campanella, Gil Hodges, Carl Erskine and Carl Furillo).

It was a team that had been managed by Wilbert Robinson, Casey Stengel, Leo Durocher and Chuck Dressen.

And now they were hiring Walt Alston?

"Walt Who?" was the general reaction around Brooklyn.

But his critics soon learned Walt would not be rattled, could not be made to feel insecure, and should not be underestimated.

He loved the game of baseball and, as it turned out, understood it and the men who played it as few have.

He was John Wayne, but he wasn't acting. But underneath that strong, silent façade lurked a mischievous sense of humor if you were one of the fortunate ones Walt opened up to.

He and Dodger executive Red Patterson once roomed together at the baseball winter meetings. Every morning, Red would step outside in his undershorts to get the morning newspaper. One morning, Walt made a quick move to the door, slammed it shut and locked it, leaving an embarrassed and angry Red out in the hallway.

Red's temperature would go up every time Walt retold the story. Walt would say, "I did let you in, Red." And Patterson would reply, "Yeah, after I banged on the door for five minutes."

Walt had plenty to smile about on the field. The Dodgers finished second in his first year as manager behind the hated New York Giants, who went on to sweep the Cleveland Indians, winners of 111 regular-season games, in the World Series.

Longtime Dodger coach Monty Basgall, Don Drysdale and Fred.

But in Walt's second year, the Dodgers not only won the pennant, but their first world championship ever. And it was all the sweeter because they did so by beating their crosstown rivals, the Yankees.

In all, Walt's teams would win seven pennants and four world championships. He would lead the Dodgers back from seventh place in 1958, the team's first year in Los Angeles, to a World Series triumph the following season over the Chicago White Sox.

And in 1963, the Dodgers, under Walt, would win yet another world championship with a four-game sweep of the Yankees. It could never get better than that.

But what I remember beyond all the glory was Walt the man. I think it was his friendship with his longtime coaches that told the most about him. During my years with the team, Alston's loyalty to longtime friends such as Red Adams, Monty Basgall, Jim Gilliam, Danny Ozark, Preston Gomez, Roy Hartsfield, Carroll Beringer and Dixie Walker was a wonderful thing to see. Walt respected his coaches, and it was clear the members of his staff felt they were working under the best manager in the game.

Alston had no problem relinquishing some of his authority. There was no ego at work there.

"Red," he would say to Adams, the pitching coach, at the start of spring training, "you take those guys this spring and you pitch them when you want to, run them when you want to, and do whatever you feel is necessary.

"But when the season starts, those guys better be ready."

And then he'd flash that Walt smile.

Yet despite the quick wit and pleasant personality, he had no interest in running with the Hollywood crowd or reaching out for commercial opportunities. That wasn't Walt.

During his years as Dodger manager, Walt let the general manager and ownership determine his coaching staff for the most part. There were three coaches who had strong personalities and plenty of ambition. Former Dodger manager Chuck Dressen was a member of Walt's staff in 1958 and 1959, and the colorful Leo Durocher, manager of both the Dodgers and rival Giants, served on Walt's staff between 1961 and 1964. Dodger general manager Al Campanis added Tommy Lasorda to Walt's staff in 1973.

Walt may not have approved of Tommy's promotion, but I never heard a word of complaint about the assignment from Walt.

In Durocher's case, complaints from Walt would have been in order, but it was just the opposite. In 1962, the Dodgers led by four games with 13 to play, but collapsed, enabling the Giants to tie them at the end of the regular season, thus forcing a three-game playoff. The Dodgers led 4-2 heading into the ninth inning of the final play-off game at Dodger Stadium, only to lose 6-4 with Dodger pitcher Stan Williams walking in the pennant-winning run.

Afterward, Durocher publicly declared he wouldn't have blown the pennant like his manager did.

An angry Buzzie Bavasi, the Dodger general manager, says he fired Durocher. But that information was never made public.

That's because the next day, according to Bavasi, Walt came to him and asked if Durocher could be hired back.

"Sure, if you want him," said Bavasi. "But why would you want him back after what he said?"

"Because," said Walt, "he's a good baseball man."

And back came Durocher.

Loved or tolerated, player or a coach, if you served under Walt, you had no doubt he was in charge. If you got under Walt's skin, he made no secret of it. If Walt liked you, he made no secret of that, either. He would jab you with that keen sense of humor and crack that granite face with a warm smile in your direction.

I remember one day during the 1970 season when there was no smile on Walt Alston's face. It was during batting practice at Dodger Stadium before a regular-season game. Walt came into the dugout, took his usual spot on the bench and casually glanced up at the lineup card, posted in its customary position above his head.

Only this time, Walt gave it a second look. And a double take.

"Roy, where's my lineup card?" he demanded of coach Roy Hartsfield, who was seated nearby.

"Right there in its regular place," said Hartsfield, trying to act nonchalant.

"That's not *my* lineup card," said Walt firmly. "That's not my writing."

"Are you sure, Skip?" said Hartsfield, squirming.

"Roy, what happened to my damn lineup card?" insisted Walt, his anger growing.

Hartsfield had run out of wiggle room.

"[Outfielder Andy] Kosco came out to see if he was starting against the lefthander tonight," Hartsfield said, "and when he saw his name wasn't in the lineup, he tore up the card."

Walt didn't have to hear anymore. He realized he was looking at Hartsfield's handwriting, realized his coach had tried to avoid a confrontation.

Walt had only one further question: "Where's Kosco?"

"I think he went back to the clubhouse," Hartsfield said.

I had been observing this whole scene unfold and, when Walt marched firmly back to the clubhouse, I figured, as the team's vice-president of public relations, I should go along. But I had no intention of getting between two guys big enough to play in the NFL.

Walt found Kosco alone in front of his locker. The Dodger manager didn't bother with small talk.

"Did you tear up my lineup card?" he asked Kosco.

Kosco nodded in the affirmative. "I did," he said. "I can't understand why I'm not starting tonight against the lefthander."

Walt moved a bit closer until he was nose to nose with Kosco.

"If you ever touch one of my lineup cards again," Walt told him, "I'll break you into so many pieces, they won't find you. Any questions?"

Two men from small towns in Ohio—Walt Alston and Fred Claire.

What could Kosco say? He knew he had foolishly stepped into Walt's domain.

"I'm sorry, Skip," was all he responded with.

Needless to say, when the Dodgers took the field that night, Kosco remained on the bench.

I've never told this story before. And I never heard Walt tell it. He didn't need to talk about how tough he was. Anyone who ever played for him knew it. And anyone who ever had problems on the field could attest to Walt's classy managerial style.

Like Willie Davis.

I remember the night Davis had a problem with a couple of balls in center field. Reporters came to Walt in his office after the game looking for critical quotes. But they had come to the wrong man.

"Willie has played great for us in center field," Walt said. "He might have gotten a bad jump or two tonight, but that's not what cost us the game. Willie Davis can play center field for me any day."

When the reporters had left, deadlines beckoning, Walt asked me to close the door. Then, his eyes narrowing, he told me, "That guy killed us out there tonight. My grandson could have caught those balls."

But angry as he was, Walt wasn't about to hang one of his players in public.

In addition to knowing the game of baseball inside and out, Walt was also excellent at cards. The common link between the two was his impressive memory. He proved highly adept at reading the cards in an opponent's hand. In baseball, I really believe he could have taken a scorecard after a game and filled it in by memory without making a mistake.

The fear of mistakes never entered into the managing process for Walt. He never stopped to think how his moves would be viewed by the media. He simply did what he thought was right.

In 1974, pitcher Don Sutton was really struggling in late summer, and the press was questioning Walt's decision to keep Sutton in the rotation. Walt never wavered, continually expressing his belief in his pitcher despite the less-than-impressive results. And, sure enough, Sutton came back strong to help pitch the team to the National League pennant and into the World Series.

Walt stuck to his personal code of conduct until the day he died. That day came 24 hours after the end of the 1984 season.

With a chance for a brief respite from the demands of baseball, Sheryl and I had made plans to fly to San Francisco, then drive to Napa for a few days of vacation.

The news hit me as we were driving across the Golden Gate Bridge. It came via the car radio: Walt Alston had passed away at 72.

I flew to Cincinnati and then drove to Darrtown where Walt was buried near the home he had built with the help of his father. And that was only a stone's throw from where Walt's father had built his own home. The beautiful, green, peaceful setting of Darrtown seemed an appropriate place for someone nicknamed "The Quiet Man" to spend all eternity.

There was an open field adjacent to the Alston home, a field where Walt and his family had played baseball on countless days. Not surprisingly, with Walt overseeing the proceedings, they took it seriously. They had uniforms, would draw lines for the base paths, and even had the national anthem played before the first pitch was thrown.

As members of Walt's family served food at the Alston home after the funeral, I gazed out a window at that field and envisioned one of those family contests going on.

Most people remember Walt in the dugout or in a conference on the pitcher's mound at Dodger Stadium or Ebbets Field. Or they remember him with one leg on the dugout steps, brow narrowed as he watched what was unfolding on the field.

My lasting image of Walt, however, is of him in Darrtown in the fading sunlight of an autumn day, brow relaxed as he watched his grandchildren, Kim and Robin, running the bases of that family field.

Postscript: A few days after I was fired, I received a wonderful letter from Kim. She wrote, "My allegiance with the Dodgers of today ended with your departure. I'll become a fan of your new ballclub."

THE BIG BOSS

Even those who could never forgive Walter O'Malley for moving the Dodgers out of Brooklyn have to admit that he forever changed major-league baseball for the better, transforming it from a regional sport to the true national pastime.

Walter always seemed to be light years ahead of everyone else, whether it was in the construction of a baseball stadium or in the burgeoning medium of pay television. But no matter his success, he never looked back, always planning for a still more exciting future. In his later years, he pursued the vision of international baseball.

Yet the sport didn't consume him. Walter always found time for his family and friends, time to play golf and pamper his prized orchids.

When he was asked by United Press International reporter Jim Cour how he would like to be remembered, Walter spun the ever-present cigar in his mouth for a moment, pondered and then replied, "I want to remembered for planting a tree."

Born in New York in 1903, Walter got a law degree from Fordham and opened a practice in Manhattan. His first link to baseball was legal work he did for the Brooklyn Trust Company, which ran the Dodger franchise after the death of owner Charles Ebbets. In 1941, Walter became the Dodger attorney. In 1944, he bought a share of the team and, in 1950, purchased control of the Dodgers.

In 1970, shortly after my arrival, Walt handed over the club presidency to his only son, Peter, and took the title of Chairman of the Board.

I remember a cartoon Walter had clipped out of a newspaper.

It showed a man sitting at a desk bearing a plate that read, "Chairman of the Board." On the outside of the door to the office was a sign hanging from the doorknob that read, "Please disturb."

It was funny, but not true. While Peter was clearly in charge, Walter still made his presence known to everybody in the organization. Energetic and driven to the end, Walter could never totally divorce himself from his Dodgers.

Some of my most interesting moments with him occurred in "Room 40," the Dodgers' executive dining room located just off the press dining room on the third level behind home plate at Dodger Stadium.

Room 40, a reference to the Bossert Hotel in Brooklyn where Dodger officials would gather for meals or social affairs, was established so that club executives didn't have to stray too far in search of lunch or dinner before a game. It also offered a convenient hideaway for front-office people in need of privacy while hashing out crucial decisions.

Walter always sat in the same chair in Room 40, positioning himself in the far corner so that he could take in all that was happening.

I always thought of it as Walter's chair, and I know that other front-office people did as well. Out of respect, none of us would ever sit in that chair, even after Walter died in 1979.

And that held true to my final day with the Dodgers.

Sitting with Walter in that room was quite an education.

I remember he was once asked, after Sandy Koufax had retired, what he would have had to pay the Hall of Fame lefthander had Koufax been around in the free-agency era.

Said Walter, "He would be my partner."

On another afternoon in Room 40, Walter told me, "Listen carefully to the lawyers and accountants. But don't let them make the decisions."

Once asked about the success of the Dodger organization, Walter had replied, "You will find Dodger executives at their offices when the phone rings. We may not be smarter than the next guy, but we will work hard."

I remember fuming as I walked back with Walter along the club level from Room 40 to our offices after lunch one day. The cause

Visiting with Walter O'Malley on the night Fred is elevated to Dodger VP.

of my anger was an article about Walter that I felt had depicted him unfairly.

"Fred," Walter told me, "never stop to get into a tiff. Keep the big picture in mind. We have too much work to do."

All these years later, I still remember a night in the early '70s when, despite the fact it was the offseason, I had to work late. I thought I was alone in my office until I became aware of eyes watching me. I looked up and there was Walter O'Malley in the doorway.

"Fred, you are doing a very good job," he said. "I've seen some things I hadn't seen before."

But along with the encouragement, Walter knew how to give a subtle poke now and then. In 1978, the Dodgers set an all-time attendance record of 3,347,845. No team had ever even drawn three million, and here we had just shattered the mark.

The morning after the regular season ended, I soared into my office on a wave of euphoria. After all, as the Dodger vice-president of public relations and promotions, I could claim at least a little credit for this remarkable achievement.

When I got to my desk, there was note to call Walter in his office.

"Fred, Mr. O'Malley would like to see you," said Edith Monak, Walter's secretary.

Well, I walked into Walter's office figuring I was in line for a nice pat on the back. Instead, Walter said to me, "Fred, couldn't you have lied just a little bit?"

I was perplexed. "I'm sorry, I don't understand," I said.

Walter repeated himself: "Fred, couldn't you have told just a little fib?"

I also repeated myself: "I still don't understand, Mr. O'Malley."

"Look, Fred," Walter explained, "we announced our season attendance at 3,347,845. If you had fudged just a little, we could have announced 3.5 million by counting some of the no-shows. The reason I say this is because we will never draw this many people again and 3.5 million sounds so much better than 3,347,845."

"Oh no, Mr. O'Malley," I said, "we will break that record next year."

"No, mark my words," he maintained, "we will never get that far again."

"I promise you we will," I insisted.

The Dodgers had just set an all-time attendance record. And the chairman of the board had called me in, the man in charge of marketing and promotions, not to say good job, but to maneuver me into issuing a promise that we would do better.

Driving home that night, playing our conversation over in my head, I had to smile. The man is something special, I thought.

Oh yes, and in 1982, we drew 3,608,881 and, the following season, 3,510,313. I had to go look those numbers up, but 3,347,845? I remember that number like I remember my phone number.

Postscript: As I look back over notes and cards I received while an employee of the Dodgers, I find that almost every significant occasion of my career was marked by a message from Terry Seidler.

All Dodger fans are familiar with Peter O'Malley, Walter's only son. But few are even aware that Walter and Kay also had a daughter, Terry.

I can't tell you how many times I walked out of Dodger Stadium to find a note on my car from Terry. I parked in spot No. 10, and she parked in No. 11.

Most of the notes were left after tough losses. How many other general managers walk out of the ballpark after a draining defeat and find a note saying, "We'll get them tomorrow night," a note signed by an owner of the team? The answer is none.

On the next-to-last day of the 1997 season, the Dodgers were in Denver, and the Giants were at home playing the Padres. Even though the Dodgers won, a Giant victory that same day eliminated us from play-off contention.

Sheryl and I walked back to the hotel with Terry.

Later that evening, I was alerted to a message at the front desk. It was from Terry, who had already left for home. It read, "Sheryl and Fred: Tomorrow would have been wonderful. Many thanks for all of your hard work and Sheryl's rooting. We had many highlights (but those darn Padres)."

That walk back from Coors Field to the hotel marked the end of Terry's involvement with the Dodgers since the team was sold before the start of the following season.

When my own involvement with the Dodgers ended on a trip to Coors Field midway through that 1998 season, I got a note from Terry and her husband, Roland.

It read simply, "We're very sorry."

CHAPTER V

NIGHTLINE
WITHOUT A LIFELINE

I t was a simple flight from Los Angeles to Sacramento. If it had been on time, Al Campanis would have been able to finish out his career with the dignity he deserved, and this book might never have been written.

But the flight was delayed, and the result was a dramatic turning point for two lives, in opposite directions, and a watershed moment in Dodger history.

The date was Monday, April 6, 1987. The Dodgers were in Houston to play the Astros in their opening game of the season. Both the Dodgers and major league baseball were marking the occasion with a celebration of a Dodger opener 40 seasons earlier on April 15, 1947, a game that proved to be a dramatic turning point in both Dodger history and the history of sports in this country. On that date, the long overdue integration of big-league baseball finally occurred when Jackie Robinson was inserted into the lineup of the Brooklyn Dodgers, thus becoming the first African-American to play in the majors.

It was a few small steps for Robinson to first base at Ebbets Field to start the game, but it was a giant leap for American society.

The producers of ABC's *Nightline* decided to commemorate the events with guests Roger Kahn, a former Brooklyn beat writer and author of *Boys of Summer*, Don Newcombe, a former Robinson teammate who subsequently endured his own hardships in breaking the color barrier, and Campanis.

Newcombe, a member of the Dodger front office, had a speaking engagement that night in Sacramento, but he agreed to do the show when he landed.

When *Nightline*'s producers learned Newcombe's flight would be late, they figured Campanis' role would expand. Nobody, however, could have imagined how much. Or how disastrously.

Al Campanis, the Dodger general manager for nearly two decades, was certainly qualified to speak at length about Jackie Robinson. He had been Robinson's roommate all the way back to 1946 when the two played for the Montreal Royals, then a Dodger affiliate in the Triple A International League.

It wasn't fate that put Al in the same room with Robinson. It was Branch Rickey, the Dodger president who was grooming Robinson to become baseball's first black pioneer. Rickey told Al his mission would be to pave the way for Robinson both on the field and off.

On the field meant Al, a shortstop, would help Robinson make the transition from that position to second base. Al explained to Robinson there were three ways to avoid a runner deliberately sliding in on him on a double play, a tactic sure to be used on Robinson even more than usual because of his color.

The stubborn Robinson told Al he'd handle the situation himself.

On a double-play attempt soon after, a runner came barreling in on Robinson and sent him flying. The second baseman was still on his back when Al came rushing over.

Robinson looked up at Al, grinned and said, "Can I start learning those other two ways tomorrow morning?"

Off the field, Al stood side by side with Robinson against the inevitable onslaught of prejudice.

A happy foursome of (back row, left to right) Fred,
Al Campanis, Peter O'Malley and (front) Tommy Lasorda.

"It wasn't easy," Al told the *Los Angeles Times* a year before his death. "Several times, I had to jump in when players said something to him about his color."

Al was born in Kos, Greece on Nov. 2, 1916, but his family moved to the New York area when he was still a youngster. It didn't take him long to fall in love with baseball.

Nor did it take him long to envision his love affair with the game culminating at the major-league level. Al reached that peak all right, but for barely long enough to get his uniform dirty. In 1943, he played in seven games for the Brooklyn Dodgers, getting two hits in 20 at-bats.

And that was it.

But that was just the beginning for Al and the Dodgers. He was determined to remain in the game in some capacity, and that passion for baseball caught Rickey's attention.

Rickey employed him in many ways other then merely as Robinson's tutor. Al played in the Dodgers' minor-league system, he coached and he managed in winter ball. When Al's career in uniform was over, he became a Dodger scout.

He was happy as long as he remained a disciple of Rickey. His admiration for the famed executive was obvious to all who came in contact with the man from Kos. I never heard Al talk about Rickey without referring to him as "Mr. Rickey."

After Rickey departed, Al continued to move up in the Dodger organization, becoming director of scouting. When executive vice-president and general manager Buzzie Bavasi left the Dodgers to become president of the San Diego Padres after the 1968 season, Al was promoted to vice-president in charge of both player personnel and scouting prior to the 1969 season.

This was truly Al's dream job, and he would have gladly kept it forever.

On the night of April 6, Al was with the Dodgers in Houston for the season opener in the Astrodome.

Contacted the previous Friday by ABC, Al, without telling anyone, agreed to do the show after the game. With play underway, Steve Brener, the Dodger publicity director, was seated in the press box when he was approached by a *Nightline* representative inquiring about Al's whereabouts. After pointing to the row behind him in the press box, Steve asked what this was all about. He was told Al had agreed to do *Nightline* after the game. Steve was surprised that, as publicity director, he hadn't been informed.

Steve was also concerned because he could see the difficulties his general manager would face. Al was a 70-year-old man who had only been in Houston a few hours after traveling there on game day. Fatigue could further cloud already confusing circumstances to someone unaccustomed to the complexities of broadcasting. Al would be placed on a stool behind home plate, staring into the camera and the glare of the bright lights without benefit of a monitor.

If I had known Al was going on the show, I would have told him the questions in all probability weren't going to relate to teaching Jackie how to make the double play. This was *Nightline*, dealing with an historical event with still important issues left unresolved 40 years later.

Dodger announcer Vin Scully looked down on the field after finishing his own broadcast and saw Al speaking into the camera.

Scully, of course, didn't know what Al was saying, or even what the subject matter was. But he thought to himself Al looked "so alone, so vulnerable."

On the air, host Ted Koppel asked about the lack of blacks in significant positions of authority in baseball.

"I truly believe they may not have some of the necessities to be, let's say, a field manager, or perhaps, a general manager," Al told Koppel and a national television audience. "Why are black people not good swimmers? Because they don't have buoyancy."

Those who knew Al expressed shock. There had never been a hint of bigotry in anything he had ever said or done.

In my view, what Al had attempted to do that night was to defend his beloved game of baseball in an area where there was no defense. He saw his sport being challenged, and he wanted to come to the rescue.

I believe the other factor that drove Al, in his answers to Koppel's questions, was that Al honestly felt there were few men, and I mean few regardless of color, who had the knowledge and ability to be general managers. Al looked upon himself as a person who had been chosen by the great Branch Rickey, and there were few so chosen.

In Atlanta, *L.A. Times* reporter Randy Harvey, on assignment, flicked on the television in his hotel room and watched the show unfold. Soon, as was the case with many viewers, his jaw dropped.

But unlike most viewers, Harvey swung into action. With the East Coast three hours ahead of the West, there was still time to get a story on Al into the next day's paper.

Harvey called his boss, *Times* sports editor Bill Dwyre, who, in turn, called Buddy Martin, sports editor of the *Denver Post*, owned by the Times Mirror Company in those days. Dwyre awoke Martin and asked him to watch the show, which would air in Denver 90 minutes ahead of L.A.

Once he had Al's comments in hand, Dwyre knew he had to run a story.

"It was the toughest decision I ever had to make," said Dwyre years later. "It was a real tough call. Part of me wished I had missed it, that I hadn't had a shot at it. But once I saw it, I did the journalistic thing. My head told me one thing, but my heart told me the opposite.

"[Campanis] is a friend of mine. To this day, I hate this story."

With the account of Al's appearance on the front page of the *Times* sports section the next morning, there was no chance it would just go away quietly.

Al didn't know about the *Times* story, didn't need to know.

When Scully came back to the hotel lobby after the *Nightline* show, Al was standing there.

"Hey roomie, what's up?" said Scully to the man who had been his roommate with the Brooklyn Dodgers back in the '50s.

"I think I screwed up," replied a chagrined Campanis.

"Oh, I'm sure it will be fine," Scully assured him, although the Dodger announcer didn't know what Al had said. "Let's go have a drink."

Al wasn't in the mood. He excused himself and went to his room, looking, in Scully's words, "so confused, so upset, pale and shaking."

The next morning, Scully and the rest of the Dodger family, myself included, learned why Al had been so unnerved.

Unaware that Al was going to be on *Nightline*, I had gone to bed in my Pasadena home a short time after the game ended and awoke to see the story in the next morning's *L.A. Times*. I can still see the placement of that story, running down the right-hand column on the front page of the sports section. I couldn't believe what I was reading.

The immediate reaction of Peter O'Malley, who had also been in Houston, was that all this would soon blow over and everything would return to normal. But Peter had misread the reaction, failing to envision the firestorm of criticism that would come at him and the Dodger organization from all directions.

It soon became apparent Al would have to be dismissed from his post as general manager. On Wednesday morning, April 8, prior to the finale of the three-games series in Houston, a day game, Al was informed he would have to resign from the job that had been the culmination of his nearly 45 years in the Dodger organization.

Peter then made one of his rare visits to the Dodger clubhouse to inform the staff and players of his decision.

Late that afternoon, just prior to boarding a flight home with Campanis, Peter called me. I had never heard him so down. His voice sounded as though he was calling from the bottom of a barrel.

"Fred," he said, "you have to take this job. I have asked Al to resign, and I need you to take this job."

I told Peter I would accept the position.

The next call came from Al, who had also not yet boarded.

"I wish you could have been with me the other night before I went on that show," Al said.

"I also want you to know one thing. Mike Brito is a very good scout."

Sadly, I replied, "I wish you had told me you were going to go on the show."

Al showed me a lot—not that I didn't already know what kind of a person he was in that I had worked with him for so long—by mentioning Brito at that time of extreme personal anguish. Al wanted me to know Brito, a key figure along with a scout named Corito Varona in the signing of pitcher Fernando Valenzuela, was a valuable member of the staff.

Brito is never bashful about his ability and his accomplishments as a scout. I believe Al felt his absence could place Mike in a vulnerable position under a new GM.

It so happens I shared Al's high regard for Mike, one of the finest scouts in the game and a key to the Dodgers' success in signing players from Mexico over the years.

But there was Al, just fired, about to board a plane with his life shaken and forever changed, and one of his first concerns was the well-being of the Dodger organization and the well-being of a scout he didn't want to see get lost in the shuffle.

Al cared for and respected his scouts, just as he did the player development people, just as he did the players, no matter the color of their skin.

Through all of the agony of his dismissal, Al never lost his love for the Dodgers or baseball. He would make frequent trips to Dodger Stadium, usually sitting on the club level. He would often come into my office to visit and talk about the game.

Prior to becoming general manager, I often had the opportunity to attend GM meetings with Al. I also sat in on his nightly meetings in spring training. His passion for the game, and the men who played it, was tremendous.

I remember receiving a call from Al one day not long after his departure from the team. During the conversation, Al mentioned he had long had a picture of Jackie Robinson in his office and, it seemed to me, he was making the point as if to say he had no prejudice.

"Al, I've known you for 20 years," I responded. "You don't have anything to prove to me. I know you."

CHAPTER VI

OUT OF A NIGHTMARE, A DREAM JOB

W ith Al Campanis having sunk under the weight of his own words and the Dodger organization rocked by waves of criticism, Peter O'Malley had asked me to assume command of the ship, and I had agreed.

But before officially taking my place on the bridge, I wanted a clarification. After having lost our first three games of the season in Houston, we were about to stage our home opener. I arrived at Dodger Stadium early that day and went to Peter's office.

"Peter, you've asked me to take this position," I said, "and I will take it under one very important condition. That is that I get full, total and complete responsibility for baseball operations. If you don't want this, and you want me to serve as part of a committee until you find a general manager, that is okay with me. But if I have the job, I want the responsibility. If I get run out of town, I want to be sure it's for the right reasons."

I knew full well that Tommy Lasorda hoped to be the GM one day and, if I had any chance at all to succeed in the job, I would have to have full authority.

Peter looked at me and smiled.

"Fred, it's yours," he said. "I wouldn't touch that job with a 10-foot pole."

I went downstairs and met with the players, telling them I would be the one making the player personnel decisions.

I told the media the same thing, adding that I would rely heavily on advice from Tommy, the coaches, the scouts, and particularly, farm director Bill Schweppe and scouting director Ben Wade.

When I was asked by Ross Newhan of the *L.A. Times* about the duration of my term as GM, I honestly replied, "I don't know if it's for one day, two days or three days. All I know is that I'll do the best I can for however long it is. Ultimately, it will be Peter's decision."

Showing amazing foresight, Newhan wrote the following in the *Times* on April 10, 1987: "Is Claire's appointment interim or permanent? Will Manager Tommy Lasorda, as often speculated, eventually become the general manager? Will Bobby Valentine, or Bill Russell, or Joe Amalfitano, or Kevin Kennedy, the highly regarded manager of the Bakersfield Dodgers, replace Lasorda in the Dodgers' clubhouse and dugout?"

Although I had been handed control of one of the most storied teams in all of sports, and understood the trust that had been placed in my hands, I wasn't intimidated by the task in front of me.

I was in the loop. I had attended all of Al Campanis' spring-training meetings that year, just as I had done in each of my previous 17 full seasons with the team.

Al always made me feel welcome and a part of the meetings. He knew there were many issues related to the news media and, since becoming a team vice-president in 1975, I had been involved in discussions regarding free agents, arbitration and the team payroll.

I felt honored to be at those meetings, which took place in the Roy Campanella room at Dodgertown, listening to Al, Walter Alston, Tommy and the coaches discuss the Dodgers in particular, and baseball in general.

So I wasn't hesitant about imposing my will on the club's fortunes in my new position. And I knew just where I needed to impose it immediately.

When the 1987 season began on that disastrous night in Houston, the Dodgers were carrying 11 pitchers, unusual in that era because most Dodger teams up to that point had a staff of 10.

It was clear to me all that spring the Dodger coaching staff had doubts about lefthander Jerry Reuss. There was concern about the way Jerry had pitched during the spring, and whether he really fit in the starting rotation. He also carried a salary of $1 million, and that salary became guaranteed with the start of the season.

Things became more complicated in my very first game as general manager, the home opener. I received a call immediately after the game from our trainer, Bill Buhler, who advised me third baseman Bill Madlock had suffered a shoulder injury that would place him on the disabled list.

I was aware that utility man Mickey Hatcher had just been released by the Minnesota Twins. I knew all about Mickey from his days with our club. Mickey had come up through our farm system and had played his first big-league game as a Dodger.

So on April 10, the morning after the opener, I called Mickey's agent, Willie Sanchez, a longtime friend who had worked in our minor-league system. Willie and I had become close when I recommended to Peter O'Malley that Willie run the 1980 All-Star Game at Dodger Stadium.

"Call Mickey," I told Willie, "and tell him to be prepared to sign a contract if we can work out a deal."

At first Willie thought I was talking about a Triple A contract at Albuquerque. I told Willie that my intention was to sign him to a Dodger contract and get him to Dodger Stadium that very night.

There was no doubt in my mind this would be a good deal for our club—sign Hatcher, who could play third base in Madlock's absence and give our team some of the spirit he always exuded, and release Reuss.

At mid-morning of my second day as general manager, I went into Peter's office for final approval.

"You want to do what?" said Peter when I told him my plan. I repeated it.

"What do we owe Reuss?" Peter asked.

"One million."

"You had better get [team general counsel] Sam [Fernandez] in here," said Peter, "to discuss this with us."

With Sam's arrival, I repeated my proposal one more time. Yes, I wanted to release a veteran pitcher who was due a $1 million buyout and sign a player who had just been released by the Twins.

"Fred, I suggest you wait until Tommy and his coaches get here later today to discuss this," Peter said.

I told Peter I was confident I knew the feelings of Tommy and the coaches based on the spring meetings and I wanted Hatcher in uniform for that night's game.

"I wouldn't move this fast, Fred," Peter said firmly. "But you're the general manager. I'll say it again. I wouldn't do this at this time, but it's your call."

I nodded.

"I understand," I said as Sam and I got up from our chairs and headed out of Peter's office.

As we walked down the hall, Sam looked at me and asked, "What are you going to do, Fred?"

"When I get back to my office I'm going to call Jerry Reuss and tell him he has been released," I said, "and then I'm going to call Willie Sanchez and sign Mickey Hatcher."

In response, Sam uttered two words: "Holy cow."

I called Sanchez, and we agreed on a deal for Hatcher. Mickey, who had been working out in Arizona, arrived in my office just as the game was getting underway. He signed his contract and quickly went down to the clubhouse to get in uniform.

In the ninth inning, Tommy called upon Mickey as a pinch-hitter with a runner on third and the Dodgers trailing the Padres by a run. Mickey hit a grounder to third base and, when the ball went through the legs of Kevin Mitchell, the tying run came in.

As the crowd went wild, the phone in my box rang.

It was Peter. "Are you having any fun?" he inquired with delight.

"Peter, we're going to win the pennant," I shouted.

I may have gotten a little carried away with my enthusiasm, but my career as the Dodger general manager was underway.

CHAPTER VII

MY MANAGER, TOMMY

T ommy Lasorda first learned about this book through Steve Springer, who also informed the Hall of Fame manager that he would be assisting me on the project.

Tommy's response? "Why does he need any assistance? I thought Fred was a writer."

Tommy also had a message for me: "Remind Fred he once played for me."

Indeed, I was a writer when I first met Tommy. And indeed, I wound up in uniform with Tommy as my manager.

My relationship with Tommy began in the spring of 1969 when he was the manager of the Dodgers' Triple A team in Spokane and I was a beat writer for the *Long Beach Independent Press-Telegram*. It ended with my sudden departure from the Dodgers.

In between, we had a bond that Tommy often described by saying, "Fred and I are as close as brothers."

It was a generally good relationship even after I became general manager at a time when Tommy already was a veteran manager with hopes of becoming a GM himself one day. The GM-manager relationship is never easy, but Tommy and I worked well together in those roles for a decade because we both had a burning desire to see the Dodgers succeed.

In my first spring with the Dodgers, my closest companion at Dodgertown was John Wiebusch, a fellow writer who worked at the *Los Angeles Times*. John and I had become friends the previous season when we had covered the Angels for our respective newspapers.

John and I soon found ourselves spending a lot of time with Tommy, even though our primary focus was on the big-league club.

Tommy had a million stories to tell, a highly entertaining manner of telling them, and, unlike some of our colleagues, John and I, as the new guys on the beat, hadn't heard those stories before.

One memorable night, Spunky Lasorda, Tommy's son, joined the three of us for dinner. Afterward, with Spunky looking for some excitement that went beyond baseball conversation, it was decided we would all go roller-skating.

I call it a memorable night because I had never before been roller-skating, and I did more falling than skating. It was fun, and Tommy and I shared laughs about the experience for years to come.

It was during dinner another evening that I mentioned to Tommy I would like to take infield practice with his Spokane team. I told him I had played high school ball at Torrance—okay, so it was for the JV team—and I wanted to put my skills on display.

A few days later, as I was preparing to board the Dodger team bus for a trip to Orlando and an exhibition game against the Minnesota Twins, I heard that booming voice that would become so familiar to all in the Dodger organization in the years to come.

"Hey, Fred! Fred!" yelled Tommy as he approached the bus in his Spokane uniform. "I thought you said you wanted to play for my team. Why not today?"

Spokane was to play on Field 2, adjacent to the Dodger clubhouse.

It's the spring of 1969 when Fred is a sportswriter and Tommy Lasorda is the manager of Spokane.

"I said I wanted to take infield," I replied. "I didn't say anything about playing in a game."

I could see in the distance Spokane about to take the field against the Single A Bakersfield club.

"Okay," Tommy said, "get on that bus, you chicken shit, and don't mention anything to me again about playing for my team."

Tommy always did know how to motivate a guy.

"Where do I get my uniform?" I said sharply, taking the challenge. Or perhaps taking the bait would be a better analogy.

"Go see Jim Muhe in the minor-league clubhouse," Lasorda said. "Tell him you want a Spokane uniform and then get back over here to Field 2."

I took one last look at the team bus and off I went to see Muhe, the longtime, much-respected visiting clubhouse man at Dodger Stadium.

I soon reported in uniform to Tommy, now my skipper, who told me to loosen up, play some catch down the right-field line and then return to the bench for duty.

After having done so, I told Tommy, "I'm ready to play."

"Go coach first base," Tommy ordered.

Now it was my turn to throw out a challenge.

"Listen, you chicken shit," I said, "I didn't come here to coach first base."

"Okay pal," said Lasorda, "next inning, you replace Bobby Valentine at shortstop."

And so I did.

As I was coming to bat for the first time, Tommy turned to National League umpire Billy Williams, watching the game from the Spokane bench, and said, "Wait until you see this guy hit. He's just out of Stanford and we paid him a $100,000 bonus."

As I got into the batter's box, the catcher looked up at me and said, "Hey, you were with the big club last year, weren't you?"

Feeling at the peak of my confidence, I shot back, "Just have the pitcher throw the ball, okay?"

Obviously the catcher had confused me with someone else. But not for long. The pitcher, a lefthander named Bob Dorn, immediately found my weakness: A fastball right over the heart of the plate. I swung and missed.

Two more fastballs and I was headed back to the bench.

Williams leaned over to Tommy and said, "You paid that guy $99,999 too much."

I remained in the lineup at short and, on my third at-bat, with the game still scoreless, I came up with catcher Steve Sogge (the former USC quarterback) at second on a double.

With both teams short of pitchers and the game in the bottom half of the inning, it was going to be called if we failed to score. So, with two out, it was left to me to at least keep Spokane alive.

Amazingly, I made contact and sent a fly ball into right field. For an instant, it appeared the ball would fall untouched, and, with Sogge going on the pitch, I would drive in the winning run.

Instead, the rightfielder made a diving catch for the final out.

Game and playing career over.

But my relationship with Tommy was just beginning.

Before he ever put a mark on a lineup card, Tommy tried making his mark on the mound. He was a pitcher for 14 professional seasons, starting at Concord, N.H., in 1945. After a two-year break for military service, Tommy spent six additional seasons in the minors before being brought up to the Brooklyn Dodgers for spot duty in 1954. In all, his major-league experience consisted of parts of two seasons with Brooklyn, and one with the Kansas City Athletics in the American League. His lifetime record in 26 games was 0-4, all four decisions coming with Kansas City.

Tommy was sent back to the minors by the Dodgers in 1955 to make room for a young rookie lefthander straight out of college named Sandy Koufax.

"I can honestly say it took one of the greatest lefthanded pitchers in baseball to knock me off that Brooklyn club," Tommy always says.

But he also likes to tell how he warned Dodger general manager Buzzie Bavasi that he was making a mistake in cutting Tommy and keeping Koufax.

When that remark inevitably draws laughter, Tommy's response is, "Yeah? How do you know what *I* would have done?"

When he realized he wasn't going to be the next Sandy Koufax, Tommy turned to scouting and then managing, successfully working his way up the Dodgers' minor-league ladder by winning five pennants in eight years. In 1970, after the Dodgers' Triple A team in Spokane, managed by Tommy, won the Pacific Coast League pennant with a 26-game cushion over its closest pursuer, Tommy was named Minor League Manager of the Year by the *Sporting News*.

Tommy further enhanced his resume in the winter with managing stints in the Dominican Republic, Venezuela and in the Arizona Instructional League.

After 23 seasons in the Dodger organization—11 as a player and four as a scout along with the eight as a minor-league manager—Tommy finally reached the big-league team as a coach under Walt Alston in 1973.

From there, his advancement moved far more quickly.

At the end of the 1975 season, the final rung up the ladder was about to be placed within his grasp. Peter O'Malley told me that he and his father, Walter, were considering making a change in Dodger managers. They were thinking of talking to Walt about retirement and passing the managerial baton to Tommy.

One of the factors at play was that Tommy was being considered by at least one other team for its managerial spot—the Montreal Expos. Montreal president John McHale had asked for and received permission from Peter to talk to Tommy.

Peter first talked to Tommy himself, making it clear the Dodgers wanted Tommy to stay.

He was in my office when he took McHale's call and turned down the opportunity to interview for the job of Expo manager.

Despite that show of loyalty, I told Peter I thought it would be better if he and his father waited another season before making the change. In my view, the Dodgers would be better served if Alston had one more season, enabling Tommy to gain more experience at the major-league level.

I'm not sure my words influenced the decision, but Alston got another year.

In September of 1976, the Reds were on their way to another National League pennant—they went on to win the title by 10 games and add a second consecutive World Series title—and the O'Malleys knew it was time to talk to Walt about retirement. This time, there would be no change in plans.

Everybody could feel it coming, including Alston.

When Allan Malamud of the now-defunct *Herald Examiner* wrote a column headlined, "It's Time For a Change," Alston uncharacteristically exploded, challenging Malamud to a fight in the hallway outside the manager's office.

If Alston was going to go out, he was going to have the final word.

But when the word came down from the O'Malleys that it was indeed time for a change, the fight in Walt quickly dissipated, relief coming over him. After 23 seasons at the helm, he had grown tired of the travel and the daily grind of major-league baseball.

On September 29, 1976, I conducted a news conference at Dodger Stadium to announce that Walt Alston was retiring as Dodger manager, to be replaced by Tommy Lasorda.

The Quiet Man was leaving, his accomplishments and character speaking for themselves.

Conducting a press conference in September of 1976 as Walt Alston steps down and Tommy Lasorda becomes Dodger manager.

No one would ever call his successor The Quiet Man, but no one could say Tommy didn't produce impressive accomplishments of his own.

They were two very different men, but they were the right men for their time to lead the Dodgers.

CHAPTER VIII

DODGER MANAGER... JOE MORGAN?

This is a moment that has never before been written about, never talked about, known by only a select few.

It was a moment the Dodgers stood at a crossroads, a moment that might have changed the lives of so many.

It was the moment Tommy Lasorda said good-bye to the Dodgers.

It was the moment Joe Morgan was targeted to replace him.

It was a moment that might have saved the career of Al Campanis.

But ultimately, it was a moment that faded as quickly as it arose.

It was just after the conclusion of the 1983 season. The Dodgers had reached the playoffs only to be eliminated in the National League Championship Series by the Philadelphia Phillies, who knocked them out by winning the best-of-five series in four games.

But despite the defeat, Tommy felt it was a good time to ask for more money. After all, he was on a roll. He had just completed his seventh season as Dodger manager and, over that span, the Dodgers had been in the postseason four times, including the World Series three times, topped off by winning the 1981 Fall Classic. Tommy was one of L.A.'s most popular sports figures and a tremendous salesman of Dodger Blue.

He was appreciative of the opportunity to manage a high-profile team, but business was business and he felt he was making a large contribution to the Dodger business.

The negotiations between Peter and Tommy dragged on, finally reaching an apparent stalemate.

A pivotal meeting was scheduled at Dodger Stadium. But, in advance of that, Peter asked me to meet with Tommy away from the stadium, to make it clear that, while we wanted him to return, there was a limit to how far we would go.

Tommy and I met for breakfast at the Bonaventure Hotel in downtown Los Angeles. I made my best pitch, but I wasn't there to get into the financial details.

I told Tommy over our meal that, in the 15 years I had known him, something from my first spring with the team, 1969, still stood out. It was the way he had treated two veteran scouts, Bert Wells and John Carey, the consideration he had shown them, the way he would make it a point to include them in his dinner plans. That, I told Tommy, was a reflection, in my mind, of how much he cared about the people in the Dodger organization.

Still, Tommy knew his fate didn't rest in my hands. Peter, like his father, was going to have the final say when it came to the manager of the Dodgers.

Tommy and I headed to Dodger Stadium, Tommy bound for Peter's office, I for mine.

Their meeting didn't take long. And when it ended, I was summoned to Peter's office, as were Campanis and scouting director Ben Wade.

Peter told the three of us that he had been unable to break the deadlock and that Tommy had decided not to sign a new contract.

The Dodgers, it appeared, were looking for a new manager.

Tommy had gone downstairs to his office next to the clubhouse to make a few calls.

There is no doubt in my mind Tommy had been approached about his interest in becoming the manager of the New York Yankees. In fact, I'm told there were discussions about a five-year contract.

Tommy, of course, was still under contract to the Dodgers. Thus, any discussions would have been informal, to say the least.

Yankee owner George Steinbrenner wasn't happy with his team's third-place finish in 1983 following a fifth-place finish the previous season. Billy Martin had managed the Yankees in '83 through a season of turmoil, with Martin suspended on two occasions by American League president Lee MacPhail.

Peter's concern, of course, was with the Dodgers and, with Tommy refusing to budge, Peter didn't waste any time getting to the next order of business. He asked the three of us for our recommendations on a replacement for Tommy.

Al went first and suggested a former Dodger player who had just completed his first season as a coach with the New York Mets— Bobby Valentine.

Now, it was my turn. I had given some thought to the subject, because I knew it was a possibility for discussion, so I wasted no time in offering my candidate—Joe Morgan.

Morgan had never managed, but he had just completed his 21st season in the majors by helping the Phillies reach the World Series.

At 40, it was clear his playing career was in its final chapter. But it was also clear Joe Morgan knew enough to write a whole book on baseball. He had always struck me as someone with a great knowledge of the game, and someone who had earned the respect of everyone in the game.

I received a second on my suggestion of Morgan from Ben and approval from Peter. Al went along with the sentiment of the group.

Technically, Joe was still under contract to Philadelphia. With Al, Ben and I remaining in the office, Peter placed a call to Phillie president Bill Giles.

Peter first warned Giles that the call was confidential. With that understanding, Peter said he was calling for permission to talk to Joe Morgan about an important position with the Dodgers.

Things were moving quickly.

As soon as Peter hung up, however, he was told Tommy was on another line. Calling from his office downstairs, Tommy asked Peter, "Is that offer still on the table?"

Told it was, Tommy said, "Then I'll take it."

Peter immediately called Giles back.

"Bill," Peter said, "the call I just placed to you never took place."

Tommy came up upstairs, signed the contract and remained the Dodger manager for another 13 seasons.

Postscript: On Dec. 16, 1983, with Tommy under contract to the Dodgers, George Steinbrenner fired Billy Martin for the third time and replaced him with Yogi Berra. Martin was given a front-office job. Three days earlier, Joe Morgan had signed a one-year contract with the Oakland A's. Joe never realized how close he came to having the opportunity to manage the Los Angeles Dodgers.

CHAPTER IX

TWISTS AND TURNS
ON THE ROAD TO GLORY

Everybody knows the 1988 season had a perfect ending for me. But what very few know is that it nearly had a disastrous beginning.

At season's end, I was named Executive of the Year by the *Sporting News*, the fifth man to win that award in our organization's illustrious history behind Larry MacPhail (1939), Branch Rickey (1947), Walter O'Malley (1955) and Buzzie Bavasi (1959).

But at the start of the season, Peter O'Malley was considering my removal from the job.

The Dodgers had finished 1987, my first season as general manager, 16 games under .500 at 73-89.

That was the same record we had the previous season, prompting an evaluation of where the organization was headed with longtime general manager Al Campanis in forced retirement.

Peter O'Malley invited me to lunch at Hillcrest Country Club, but golf was the last thing on his mind. Peter told me he appreciated the dedication I had shown in replacing Al at the beginning of 1987, but he wanted me to know he was thinking of bringing in a "more experienced" person as general manager.

I told Peter I could understand his thinking on this subject, but I had treasured every minute I had served as the GM and I wanted to continue in that capacity.

"If you decide to make a change, I may go fishing in Montana for a while," I told him.

"You may do what?" Peter said.

I told him I didn't want my statement to sound like a threat, but if he was going to make a change, I wanted to take some time and think about what was best for me. Again, I reassured Peter I realized nothing was more important than the baseball operation of the team and I understood his position.

Peter didn't launch a great search for my replacement, but he did call the New York Mets and asked for permission to speak to Joe McIlvaine, who was being groomed to replace Frank Cashen as their general manager.

The Mets denied O'Malley that permission.

"I was never told Peter had called the Mets to ask for permission to speak to me," McIlvaine says today. "The only thing I knew about an interest by the Dodgers was that I was going through an airport in Los Angeles a number of years later and ran into Peter. He told me he had called the Mets and added, 'You'll never know how close you came to being the general manager of the Dodgers.'"

Once he was refused the right to pursue McIlvaine, Peter decided to stick with me. On October 6, 1987, the announcement was made that Tommy and I would be back in the manager-GM roles for 1988.

At the time, I didn't fully realize how close I had come to heading off to Montana.

Given an opportunity to return as GM, I chose to look ahead, and what I saw was a lot of work to be done. The first order of business was the winter meetings, to be held in Dallas in December.

We had three pressing needs if we were going to bounce back— a reliable shortstop, a consistent closer and left-handed help in the bullpen.

Mariano Duncan had made 21 errors in only 67 games at short-stop in 1987. We had rushed Mariano to the big leagues two years earlier to fill a need and he had done a good job, considering his lack of experience, but it was time for us to make a change.

We simply didn't have a stopper in the bullpen, an ongoing problem for our club as the numbers clearly showed. Alejandro Pena and Matt Young had tied for the team lead in saves in 1987 with 11 each. The previous year, our leader was Kenny Howell with 12 saves.

We hadn't had a closer with more than a dozen since Tom Niedenfuer had 19 in 1985 (yes, the year Tom gave up Jack Clark's home run to eliminate us in the National League Championship Series against the St. Louis Cardinals).

Our left-handed relief had been questionable even longer. We had been searching for an answer since 1983 when Steve Howe saved 18 games, but spun out of control due to drug problems.

So I came to the winter meetings for the first time as the man in charge of the Dodgers' baseball operations with a long shopping list.

I had made it clear we were willing to deal, and word spread quickly that we would entertain offers for pitcher Bobby Welch.

When those offers didn't soon turn into a deal, questions were raised. Why hadn't a GM with a prize starting pitcher been able to pull the trigger? Was it because of his inexperience? The answer was whispered through the halls of the Anatole Hotel where the meetings were being held: "Fred is afraid to make a move."

I later learned a couple of my fellow general managers were doing the whispering that my inexperience had turned the trade winds into a dead calm.

Soon, that speculation found its way into the headlines. The story was that one man—Fred Claire—was holding up the entire winter meetings as far as trades were concerned. Very frankly, I found this perception strange because I didn't see it as a chess game where everyone else was simply waiting to see me make a move.

I wasn't afraid to make a move, I just wanted to make the right move.

The Toronto Blue Jays had a real interest in Welch, but I got the feeling we were being strung along after we waited and waited for a late-evening meeting with Toronto GM Pat Gillick, only to be told by Blue Jay scout Al La Macchia that Gillick had gone to bed early. If we weren't being strung along, we certainly had experienced a breakdown in communication.

We had also been having extensive discussions with the Oakland A's and the Mets with Welch as the centerpiece of those negotiations. The night the Blue Jay meeting misfired, we held extensive talks with both the A's and the Mets.

The final meeting took place in my suite with Oakland general manager Sandy Alderson heading the A's negotiating team (which included Bob Watson, a future GM learning the ropes). Our group included Lasorda, farm director Charlie Blaney, and scouts Mel Didier and Jerry Stephenson.

As the night wore on, the following proposal was hammered out: The Dodgers would receive shortstop Alfredo Griffin and closer Jay Howell from the A's and left-handed relief specialist Jesse Orosco from the Mets. The A's would get Welch and fellow pitcher Matt Young from us, and we would send minor-league pitcher Jack Savage to the Mets.

Finally, by 3 a.m., this blockbuster, three-team deal hung on our willingness to give up Savage, a righthander whom the Mets had requested late in the negotiations. McIlvaine had seen Savage pitch in Double A ball and liked his arm.

"We can't give Savage up," said Tommy.

"Yes, we can, Tommy," I said. "We didn't come this far to let Jack Savage stand in the way of this deal."

I knew about Savage from one of our scouts, Ohio-based Carl Lowenstein. Carl had spotted Savage at the University of Kentucky. When I had been in Cincinnati the previous season, Carl had given me the rundown on Savage: Good arm, but trouble with the breaking ball.

The most important call of all in regard to that deal had already been made a month earlier by me to Reggie Otero, a Dodger scout. It was a call to invite Reggie to dinner.

That was at the GM meetings in Florida. At those meetings, I would usually seek out Oakland's Alderson. Sandy was a good jogging companion, and you always gained something when you engaged him in conversation.

As it turns out, we were a little too engrossed in our discussion during this particular run and got lost. When we finally got back to our hotel, I walked into the lobby to find Reggie waiting for me. As always, he was neatly dressed, and I stood before him dripping in sweat and apologizing for being late.

I had asked Reggie to drive from his home in Hialeah, Fla. because I wanted to ask him about Griffin. After all, Reggie had signed Alfredo to a contract in 1973 when the talented shortstop from the Dominican Republic was 16 years old.

The key part of my discussion with Alderson had focused on one aspect of the deal: Welch to the A's, Griffin to the Dodgers.

At dinner, my question to Otero, a wonderful man with a lifetime experience in baseball, came down to a single question—"Reggie, would you give up Bobby Welch in a deal that would bring us Alfredo Griffin?"

"Fred, I'd do it," said Reggie without hesitation. His absolute confidence in Griffin never left my mind during those long discussions at the meetings in Dallas.

When the Dodgers defeated the Oakland A's on the night of October 20, 1988, with Griffin as our shortstop, Reggie went to bed a happy man, knowing the contribution he had made to our championship.

Reggie never awoke from his night's sleep. He passed away at his home in Hialeah at the age of 73.

There are those who say the Dodgers were lucky to win a world championship in 1988. I take a different view. I say the victory was a tribute to men like Reggie Otero.

We made the deal and the next morning at breakfast, I looked over to the table where Gillick and La Macchia were seated and I couldn't help but wonder how they felt when hearing of the deal.

It proved to be good for everyone involved, because all three teams ended up in postseason play.

The press reviews of the rare three-way trade were mixed, but there was a telephone call that helped explain the jabs directed my way by the media during the meetings. The call came from McIlvaine.

"Fred," he told me, "I want you to know we turned up a little heat on you in the press in the hopes that we could help pave the way for a deal for Welch. If you want me to call your [local] press and give this background information, I will."

I thanked Joe for his call and told him it showed me a lot about his character. I told him his offer was greatly appreciated, but no further calls were necessary.

There was still much to do. Five days after the winter meetings, we signed A's outfielder Mike Davis. In January of 1988, we signed veteran pitcher Don Sutton for his second tour of duty with us, and the player who was to make the biggest difference for us that season—outfielder Kirk Gibson. We also signed catcher Rick Dempsey to a minor-league contract.

Whereas we had pursued Davis, Sutton and Gibson as free agents, Dempsey came to the main office at Dodger Stadium after the 1987 season and asked to see me. Due to some miscommunication between the switchboard operator and my secretary, Rosie Gutierrez, Rick waited in the lobby for nearly two hours before I had a chance to see him. I think he would have waited all night. Rick wanted to sign with the Dodgers. The minor-league contract he put his name on came with the understanding he would be given a chance to make the team in spring training.

The signing of Kirk had more turns and twists than a spy novel. During the course of the winter meetings, I held a number of discussions with Detroit Tiger general manager Bill Lajoie in hopes of working out a Gibson-for-Pedro Guerrero trade.

Guerrero had been a productive power hitter for us, but he had suffered a serious injury to his left knee in 1986, and since then, it had been getting tougher for him to move in the field. I liked Pedro, but I didn't see him as the type of player we could expect to be the leader of a championship team.

Kirk's contractual situation was clouded by the Players' Association's 1985 collusion suit against the owners. At the time of the meetings, arbitrator Thomas Roberts had yet to rule. It made for a confusing situation, because Lajoie didn't know whether Kirk would be under contract to the Tigers in 1988 or if he would be a free agent. For that matter, we were talking about trading for a player who might ultimately be set free from his contract.

We proposed a deal whereby we would trade Guerrero for Gibson but, if Kirk was declared a free agent, Guerrero would be returned to us, or we would receive players of comparable value.

When Bill walked into my hotel suite for what proved to be our final meeting on the subject, we had Dodger attorney Sam Fernandez on the speakerphone from Los Angeles to help guide us through possible pitfalls caused by the collusion case.

Bill seemed taken aback that a lawyer's viewpoint would be needed in a baseball deal. He had been with Detroit for 20 years and was the general manager who had assembled the Tigers' world championship team of 1984. An outstanding baseball man, he had never before needed a lawyer present to do a deal. But these were different times for baseball.

The morning following our meeting with Lajoie, I had a message waiting on my hotel telephone when I awoke. It was from Bill.

"I think we should let things cool off for awhile," he said. "Let's wait and see what Roberts does with his ruling."

I had no chance to make another pitch. Bill had already caught an early flight from Dallas back to Detroit.

On January 22, 1988, as a result of the Players' Association's collusion suit, Roberts declared seven players "no-risk" free agents until March 1, giving them a chance to sign with other clubs despite their existing contracts.

The seven were Gibson, Carlton Fisk, Donnie Moore, Joe Niekro, Butch Wynegar, Tom Brookens and Juan Beniquez. We had an interest in only one—Kirk Gibson.

Two days after Roberts' ruling, I was on the phone with Kirk's agent, Doug Baldwin. Doug told me Kirk was in Florida, but that he was aware of our interest and he was "ready, willing and anxious" to discuss a deal.

Baldwin said there were four key points for Kirk:

—He wanted to know his projected role and where he would hit in the lineup.

—He was interested in a two-year extension or a three-year contract and a no-trade clause.

—He first wanted to speak to Steve Sax, a friend, about the Dodgers.

—He wanted to know about the language in our guaranteed contracts (particularly as related to strike and lockout provisions).

A visit with Kirk Gibson on the day he is
introduced as a member of the Dodgers.

Kirk also had definite thoughts about the dollar structure of the deal. He wanted "in the area of $4.8 million for the next three seasons," according to Baldwin, and Kirk wanted a large signing bonus with a decreasing payout over the three seasons. Doug then proceeded to make the opening offer—a $1.5-million signing bonus, $1.3 in 1988, $1 million in 1989 and $800,000 in 1990.

Exactly one week after Roberts' ruling and too many telephone calls with Baldwin to count, Kirk Gibson agreed to sign with the Dodgers. He received a three-year contract for $4.5 million—a $1.5-million signing bonus and $1 million a year for 1988, 1989 and 1990.

We refused to give in on the no-trade clause, explaining the Dodgers never had given this provision to any player.

I called Kirk to welcome him to the team and was thrilled to hear the enthusiasm in his voice.

"I'm excited about being a Dodger," he said. "I'm excited about changing leagues. I know it's a challenge. The way I play, no one will ever accuse me of not playing hard."

An arbitrator's ruling on collusion had set Kirk free, and he had become a Dodger.

One thing was certain about my first offseason as general manager—no one was going to accuse our organization of being involved in collusion. Peter had given me the green light regarding free agents, and I made strong runs at both New York Yankee pitcher Dave Righetti and Minnesota Twin third baseman Gary Gaetti. We did everything possible to sign them, but both players ultimately decided to stay with their respective teams.

Quite frankly, the agents for both players literally ran away from our aggressive approach.

The Righetti negotiations with agent Bill Goodstein would have to rank as the most bizarre in my time as general manager. The discussions began on December 1. Three days later, we offered Righetti a two-year contract for a total of $2 million.

Goodstein refused to respond to the offer, asking to put it on hold because the winter meetings were getting underway. We refused. We didn't want to have a deal on the table while we were contemplating moves at the meetings.

Nevertheless, we resumed discussions with Goodstein after the meetings, but five days later, with the deadline nearing for Righetti to accept or reject a Yankee offer of arbitration, we still couldn't get the agent to respond to our two-year offer. He wouldn't even make a three-year proposal after he had indicated that might create a deal.

There were times when Sam and I would put Goodstein to the test to respond with a definite answer and the phone line would go dead.

Quite often, the next call would be from Ken Gurnick of the *L.A. Herald-Examiner*. Ken seemed to be quite up to date on the details of the negotiations.

Goodstein obviously was playing games and, on December 19, Righetti made the decision to accept the Yankees' arbitration offer.

The Gaetti case wasn't as strange in that Sam and I were dealing with an experienced agent in Jim Bronner.

We offered Gaetti a two-year contract worth $2.3 million on January 5, 1988.

The next day, Bronner called back and indicated Gaetti was looking for a three-year deal at $925,00 per season with a $2 million signing bonus. I asked Bronner if this was a firm offer and, if accepted, would it make Gary a Dodger? Bronner replied he could have said yes to this question the previous night, but now would have to call Gary again for a final answer.

The next day, I got a call from Bronner. Gary Gaetti had decided to stay with the Twins.

It was January of 1988 and we had been through a whirlwind of negotiations since the end of the previous season. We had lost out on Righetti and Gaetti, but had added Kirk Gibson, Alfredo Griffin, Jay Howell, Jesse Orosco, Mike Davis and Rick Dempsey.

In 1987, we had picked up Mickey Hatcher, John Shelby, Tim Belcher, Danny Heep and Mike Sharperson.

We were going to be a different team in 1988, but nobody could have predicted how different.

CHAPTER X

1988:
FROM PRANK TO PINNACLE

There is a baseball resting in a place of honor in the office of my Pasadena home. One single baseball representing enough memories to last a lifetime.

The baseball was given to me by Rick Dempsey moments after the Dodgers had clinched the 1988 world championship.

I had entered the Dodger clubhouse in Oakland following our 5-2 victory over the A's that gave us the World Series in five games. I should say I had floated into the clubhouse. I don't recall my feet touching the ground.

The celebration was already underway. Champagne corks were exploding with the contents of the bottles being sprayed in every direction. It was truly a moment to savor.

No sooner had I entered the clubhouse than I was wrapped in a bear hug by Dempsey.

"Fred, this belongs to you," he said as he pulled a baseball out of his back pocket and presented it to me. It was the ball Orel Hershiser had delivered to Dempsey to strike out Tony Phillips to end the game.

With that ball nestled tightly in his glove, Dempsey had rushed to the mound to lift a joyful Hershiser off the ground.

What were the odds of Rick Dempsey catching the final pitch in a World Series victory? The season before he had batted .177 for the Cleveland Indians. His career nearly ended when Bo Jackson plowed into him at home plate late in that season.

For that matter, what were the odds of Fred Claire receiving the World Series trophy along with manager Tommy Lasorda and team owner Peter O'Malley?

Just a longshot, you say. Just a one-in-a-million season?

I think not. I think it was the result of an amazing amount of work by an organization that bounced back after finishing 16 games under .500 in each of the two previous seasons.

It was the result of talented players who rose to the occasion, determined to succeed.

It was the work of a scouting department and a player development department that never lost track of the ultimate goal.

It was the result of a great job of managing by Tommy, supported by his coaching staff and the medical staff.

Most importantly, it was the financial and emotional support of Peter and his sister, Terry Seidler, that enabled the Dodgers to climb out of the abyss of April 1987, and make it all the way to the peak of October 1988.

The foundation for triumph in the Fall Classic was established that spring in Dodgertown. The team's season-long attitude was to be shaped before the very first exhibition game was played.

With so many new players on the club, the early days of spring training were devoted to just getting acquainted. There was a new shortstop, veteran Alfredo Griffin, who was learning to work with his second baseman, the hyper Steve Sax. There was Kirk Gibson in left field, already under the microscope as media and players alike examined his capacity for leadership. There was Mike Scioscia, who, as the catcher, felt a responsibility to make sure all the new pieces fit.

And then there was Pedro Guerrero, who had been our primary power hitter the previous half-dozen seasons. The start of spring training always meant the focus was on Guerrero, but not because of what he did on the field. Rather, it was on when he would get on the field. The beat writers always had a "Pedro Watch," placing bets on what date the usually late Guerrero would show up at Dodgertown.

But this spring, with so many new players on hand, Guerrero flew in under the radar. What interest he drew was over where he would play. He had been moved back and forth from the outfield to third base, but, as spring training moved along, Guerrreo settled in at third.

Then came opening day of the Grapefruit League for the Dodgers. It's a time to test the arms and legs, search for that familiar batting groove and generally ease into a season that stretches for the next seven months and, hopefully, longer.

With opening day of the regular season still more than a month away, it's not a day for momentous events.

But this day at Holman Stadium in Dodgertown was different. It was a promising sign that this season was to be different.

It began with Kirk Gibson, as did so many momentous moments in 1988.

Decked out in his new, sparkling white Dodger uniform, Kirk went into the outfield to run wind sprints. Power in motion, he ran with such force that his blue Dodger cap came flying off.

Were the fans seated nearby impressed? It didn't seem so, because their only response was laughter.

Kirk couldn't understand that reaction until he reached up to his forehead and eye-black, that thick, greasy material used by athletes to deflect potentially blinding rays of the sun, came off in his hand. Then, he understood. A joke had been played and it was on him. Kirk wasn't laughing.

He stormed into the Dodger clubhouse and called me in the press box. Kirk told me he was headed home for the day, but wanted to address the team the next morning. He was still furious.

The next morning at a team meeting arranged at his request, Kirk delivered a short, but powerful speech. He told his new teammates he didn't know what they were all about, but the only reason *he* had become a Dodger was to win. He wasn't there to mess around.

One other thing: He wanted to know who put the eye-black in the liner of his cap.

Jesse Orosco, our new lefthander, confessed.

After one game in the spring, Kirk Gibson had assumed control of the Dodger clubhouse.

When Kirk had been in Los Angeles for the announcement of his signing in January, he had told me at dinner one night that, "I might have to kick some butt." I had looked at him and replied, "Why do you think you're here?"

While I expected much from Kirk, I knew he didn't have to carry the entire load on his shoulders. We had holdover position players such as Scioscia, Sax, John Shelby, Mickey Hatcher and others who were also gamers. Our pitching staff was made up of a strong group of competitors.

They balanced out others like outfielder Mike Marshall, who could be moody. Or Guerrero, who loved to swing the bat, but would drive me crazy when he would make his way down the runway to the dugout with a cup of coffee in one hand and a cigarette in the other.

I believed in Pedro as a pure hitter, but I didn't believe he was the guy to carry the banner for our team or, for that matter, even for the young players from his homeland, the Dominican Republic.

The eye-black incident was only the beginning for Kirk, who remained serious and passionate all spring. He was determined in the exhibition games to show the other clubs—particularly the National League teams—that he meant business. Kirk would slide into second base in a spring contest like it was the seventh game of the World Series.

Second baseman Jeff Treadway was a second-year player with the Cincinnati Reds in the spring of 1988. When we acquired Jeff a few years later, he told me word had quickly made its way through the Florida training camps that spring that Kirk was out to upend every middle infielder in his path.

Kirk kept right on running once the 1988 season got underway, a man on a mission.

He was something. I'll never forget standing with Sheryl and Kirk's mother as we waited for the players to exit the clubhouse in Montreal and board the team bus in the runway underneath the stadium. Here came Kirk, wearing an expensive suit, hair slicked back with sunglasses that couldn't hide the look of a very confident man.

"He really thinks he's hot stuff, doesn't he?" said Kirk's mother.

Only a loving mother could put Kirk in his place.

Then again, he was hot stuff.

Everyone remembers Hershiser was the Cy Young Award winner and our starting pitcher in the final game of the World Series, but you probably could win a bet by naming the Dodgers' Opening Day starter for 1988. It was Fernando Valenzuela, still worthy of the honor.

We didn't get off to a great start, opening the season on April 4 at Dodger Stadium with a 1-0 loss to the Giants.

For Fernando, things would only get worse. After six consecutive seasons of working 250-plus innings, he experienced shoulder problems in late June and was placed on the disabled list for the first time in his career on July 31. Fernando missed all of August, coming back to pitch only seven innings the rest of the way. He was not healthy enough to be considered for postseason play. He finished 5-8 after averaging 16 wins over the previous seven seasons.

During a year remembered as one where everything went right for the Dodgers, few remember we lost our ace pitcher early on.

Just as Gibson assumed the role of team leader, Orel took over Fernando's role as the ace.

1988 award winners— (back row, left to right)Tommy Lasorda, Kirk Gibson, Fred, Tim Belcher, Tim Leary and (kneeling) Orel Hershiser.

The other pieces fell into place. A team is only as strong as it is up the middle. We had Scioscia, an immovable rock, behind the plate and a much-improved defense in both the infield, Griffin smoothly blending with Sax, and in the outfield, where Shelby had an outstanding year in center with his glove.

Our power was to come from the outfield with Gibson hitting 25 home runs and driving in 76 in an MVP season; Shelby adding 10 homers and 64 RBIs; and Marshall contributing 20 homers and 82 RBIs.

Sax got us started at the top of the lineup with his hustle and speed. He also kept everyone on the team loose with his great sense of humor and personality.

It was the group known as the "Stuntmen"—our players coming off the bench—who added the final, crucial element in a season in which we won 94 games. The Stuntmen consisted of Dempsey, the irrepressible Hatcher, who was to become a World Series hero, Dave Anderson, who took over at shortstop in late May when Griffin injured his right hand, and the always cool and collected Mike Sharperson, along with Franklin Stubbs, Tracy Woodson and Danny Heep.

Stubbs went from Stuntman to starter, winding up with the most games at first base (84) after breaking out of a group of seven players battling for that spot. Jeff Hamilton ended up as our primary third baseman, taking over for Guerrero.

But with all these elements contributing as they did, the end result wouldn't have been possible without the most important element, our pitching. We had a team ERA of 2.96 and led the National League in complete games (32), shutouts (24) and saves (49). Orel led the way with 23 wins, Tim Leary had 17 and rookie Tim Belcher had 12.

Orel enjoyed an incredible season that just kept building and building. In his last start of the regular season in San Diego, he pitched 10 shutout innings to extend his consecutive-innings scoreless streak to 59, breaking Don Drysdale's major-league record by one-third of an inning.

Jay Howell was the leader in the bullpen with 21 saves, Alejandro Pena recording 12 and Orosco nine.

And I can't forget the contributions of two unsung performers on the mound, Don Sutton at the beginning of the season and John Tudor in the stretch run.

It might seem funny to refer to a Hall of Famer like Sutton as an unsung hero, but, at that stage of his career, 22 years after his rookie season, not a lot was expected of him by some.

*The Claires share a ride with Mickey Hatcher and family in
the parade honoring the 1988 world champion Dodgers.*

With the trade of Bobby Welch, I had signed Don in January,
the announcement arousing some critical comment by writers.

Steve Bisheff of the *Orange County Register* asked this question
in his column of January 7: "If the Angels, with only one proven,
able-bodied, full-time starter heading into spring training, no longer
deemed it necessary to employ Sutton's services, why would the Dodgers even be interested? Are they trying to fool us? Or themselves?"

Quite honestly, I wasn't trying to fool anyone. I was fully aware
that Don would be pitching at 43 years of age, his hair as gray as
mine, only permed.

I also knew he was one of the great Dodger pitchers of all time and he would come into spring training and show every pitcher on our staff—particularly the younger guys—how to prepare for a season with a great work ethic. Don had learned such preparation by watching and working with people like Don Drysdale, Sandy Koufax and Claude Osteen.

Sutton started 16 games for us that season, winning three. The highlight for him was a 4-0 shutout over the Chicago Cubs on April 27 with Pena getting the save.

Don's final start came on August 9 in Cincinnati after he had returned from a one-month stint on the disabled list due to a sprained right elbow. We lost to the Reds 6-0 and, after the game, I met with Tommy Lasorda in his office in the visiting clubhouse.

Tommy was adamant that Don could no longer help us, and I agreed it was time to make a move. We decided to bring Ramon Martinez up from Albuquerque to replace Don in the rotation.

Don had been the role model we expected him to be in the spring, and had given us a veteran presence during much of the season while Martinez gained experience at triple-A. But now, it was time to make the switch.

I met with Sutton the following day and told him of my decision. It wasn't easy, I said, because of his many contributions to the Dodgers. But, in my opinion, it was necessary.

I gave him an option. If he elected to announce his retirement, we would make the announcement in that fashion.

Don wanted to know if a retirement decision would include a guarantee he'd continue to be paid for the rest of the season.

I told him that just wasn't possible. It would set a bad precedent, in my mind, to pay off the contract of a retiring player. Sorry, I told Don, the only way you will be paid is if you are released.

So he asked for his release.

In retrospect, I have to admit it was a mistake on my part. At the time, dealing with Little D, as Sutton was known early in his career, I was thinking of Big D, Don Drysdale. When Drysdale announced his retirement in August of 1969, he was not paid for the remainder of that season.

Even so, with only a couple of months to go, I should have backed off the point and enabled Sutton to announce his retirement as opposed to giving him his release.

When we won the World Series, I made a point to invite Don and his wife, Patti, to be our guests for our visit to the White House, and I even joined them for breakfast one morning on the trip.

Even so, I have the feeling Don never forgave me for the way his departure was handled, and, quite frankly, I don't fault him for his feelings.

In mid-August, we were holding on to a narrow lead in the West Division, a lead we had held since May 26, but it was clear we would need a veteran pitcher if we were to prevail.

With Fernando on the DL, we had an all right-handed starting staff, so it was crucial that the veteran be a southpaw. The pitcher we targeted was lefty John Tudor of the Cardinals.

After a number of conversations with Cardinal GM Dal Maxvill, we traded Guerrero for Tudor on August 16. Tudor was leading the N.L. with a 2.29 ERA at the time.

I informed Pedro of the trade in Tommy's office at Dodger Stadium prior to a game, and the veteran slugger broke down in tears. It was no wonder. He had joined our organization in 1974 at the age of 17, as the result of a trade with Cleveland, and had been with us ever since. So I could certainly understand his emotions.

The trade worked out well for Pedro. With free agency pending for him at season's end, his agent, Tony Attanasio, was able to get him a three-year contract with the Cardinals for $6.2 million.

Talk about radical change. In a period of slightly more than two weeks, beginning July 31, Fernando Valenzuela had gone on the disabled list for what amounted to the remainder of the season; Sutton had been released, and Guerrero, the team's top slugger for several seasons, had been traded.

But we were still on top.

We had been fueled earlier by a wave of momentum that began in Chicago in mid-July. We held a two-game lead with a record of 48-36 when we entered Wrigley Field on July 14 after the All-Star break. We swept the Cubs in five straight games and departed Chicago with a lead of seven games as we soared to 17 games over the .500 mark.

As Gibson made his way off the field at Wrigley after the final game and raced up the old wooden stairs to the small visiting clubhouse, he kept shouting, "What a f........team! What a f........team!"

Our lead had dropped to just a half-game when Sutton made his final start in the loss at Cincinnati, but Tudor joined us a week later and won four of his nine starts.

We were not to be caught and ended up winning the National League West by seven games.

Only two NL teams held an advantage over us during the regular season. The Mets dominated us with 10 wins in 11 games, and the always pesky San Diego Padres took 11 of 18 games. And wouldn't you know it, we had to face the Mets in the National League Championship Series.

We equaled our season victory total against the Mets by splitting the first two games of the NLCS. And we were ahead 4-3 in the bottom of the eighth inning of Game 3 on a cold and overcast day at Shea Stadium with our closer, Jay Howell, on the mound.

Suddenly, Met manager Davey Johnson emerged from his dugout and approached home plate umpire Harry Wendelstedt.

"Take a look at his glove," Johnson told Wendelstedt, pointing toward Howell.

The veteran umpire went to the mound, examined Jay's glove and ejected him from the game.

The next three relievers gave up four runs and the Mets won 8-4. As Howell departed and the Mets mounted their rally, the fans began to chant, "Dodgers cheat! Dodgers cheat!"

I have seldom been so upset in my entire life as I sat in the field boxes with my wife, Sheryl, Peter and Annette O'Malley and Terry Seidler, watching this scene play out. At that point, I wasn't sure what Wendelstedt had discovered on Jay's glove, but my anger increased with every passing moment. Quite frankly, I felt terrible for Peter and Terry to be sitting there, after all of their heartfelt efforts, hearing fans yell, "Dodgers cheat!"

When the game ended, I stormed into Tommy's office and asked him to have pitching coach Ron Perranoski join us.

"I don't know what the hell happened out there today, but I have only one thing to say," I told them. "No matter what happened, the only thing I want said by everyone on this team is the absolute truth."

As it turned out, Wendelstedt had discovered pine tar on the heel of Jay's glove. "Guys have been using it for a million years," Jay said later. "Most hitters don't give a shit. They don't care about pine tar. They don't like spitballs or scuffed balls."

Having already made arrangements for Sheryl to go back to the Grand Hyatt, our team hotel, I decided to take the team bus back. After waiting for the players and staff to shower and dress, I waited still longer on the bus because Tommy had disappeared. Finally, I was informed Tommy had already gone back to the hotel by car.

My temperature, already close to the boiling point, inched up even higher. I couldn't understand why Tommy hadn't sent word he had a ride back to the hotel instead of keeping the players and staff waiting.

When I walked into the lobby of the Grand Hyatt, there was Tommy standing with a group of people. I approached him and said, "Thanks a lot for keeping all of us waiting. That was great of you."

My anger was obvious as I turned and headed to my room. I realized I had overreacted, but the sequence of events that day had been more than I could handle.

Early the next morning, I received a call from Tommy, asking if he could come to my room. When we met, he told me he was hurt and disappointed by the way I had approached him. He apologized for the mixup related to the bus.

"It was a tough day for all of us," I replied. I, in turn, apologized to Tommy for overreacting.

We were down 2-1 to the Mets in the NLCS and Howell received a two-game suspension, but at least we were all back on the same page.

A remarkable ninth-inning home run by Scioscia off Dwight Gooden enabled us to tie the series at two and we took the NLCS in seven games, Hershiser winning the clincher at Dodger Stadium with a 6-0 shutout.

The victory swept us into the World Series and, as the history books have well documented, we won the first game over Oakland and took the momentum for the remainder of the series on Gibson's ninth-inning, pinch-hit home run at Dodger Stadium.

It was to be Gibson's only at-bat in the World Series, but it provided one of the most memorable moments in the history of the Fall Classic.

As Kirk rounded the bases, I left my box on the club level and began to walk back to my office. It was a strange feeling because, while a sellout crowd departing at the end of a game would normally pack that club level, there was nobody to be found in my path. Every-

A championship moment for Peter O'Malley, Fred and Tommy.

one was still standing and cheering and wishing that moment would last forever.

I know the feeling.

Postscript: You will find a few special books on baseball in my office, including Gibson's, which is entitled Bottom of the Ninth. *Kirk provided this inscription: "To Fred Claire: You are Mr. Dodger. I thank you for believing in me. Kirk Gibson"*

CHAPTER XI

CALLED STRIKE: GAME OUT, REPLACEMENT PLAYERS IN

T here were no major league games played between August 12, 1994 and April 24, 1995. And yet during that period, the game was forever changed.

It was the period when a 232-day player strike wiped out the 1994 World Series and spawned replacement players for 1995.

It was a period of bitterness and division between owners and players, and anger and alienation among fans.

If ever there was a lose-lose situation for baseball, this was it.

The 1994 season opened without a contract between the owners and players. The owners were insisting a salary cap was necessary for survival, because, they said, free agency and salary arbitration were killing the game.

The dispute over a Collective Bargaining Agreement was nothing new for baseball. The only thing different this time was the resolve of the owners to change a system that had resulted in a dramatic increase in player salaries, and a greater division between the payrolls of large- and small-market teams.

While the issues may have changed somewhat through baseball's years of labor unrest, the outcome never seemed to vary. The owners would change their negotiating leaders, but, nevertheless, would usually cave in at the bargaining table. The Players' Association would maintain consistency in leadership, Marvin Miller eventually passing the baton to Don Fehr, and get most of its demands satisfied.

When Fehr and the union set a strike date of August 12, 1994, the players fell in line. They weren't about to argue with a leadership group that kept producing positive results.

On August 11, the Dodgers were in Cincinnati where Ramon Martinez pitched a 2-0 shutout over the Reds to give us our second win in a row in the series and a three and a half game lead in the National League West.

No one, not owners, players or negotiators, would have dared predict it at the time, but that was to be our last game of the season.

There was little celebrating in our clubhouse as the players packed their bags to head for their individual homes. At a time when our team had come together to make a run for postseason play, we found ourselves headed in different directions. Celebrating a victory had been replaced by contemplating a stalemate.

When the deadlock remained unbroken and the World Series was canceled for the first time in 92 years, fans across the country swore they were finished with baseball.

As the 1995 season approached, the owners, determined to gain control of the situation, told their teams there would be a season, with or without the striking players. If necessary, according to a mandate from the Commissioner's Office, we were to be prepared to take the field with replacement players.

The spring of 1995 was to be a spring like no other in the history of major league baseball.

I had no interest in putting a group of players in Dodger uniforms who were not the best we could locate. If we were going to play even one National League game that could determine our place in the standings, I had every intention of winning that game. As the general manager, I had no interest in putting bartenders, truck drivers or softball players in uniform as some people seemed to be suggesting.

We soon discovered that finding capable players who weren't already under contract to a big-league organization was frustrating and unproductive. Even minor league players who were unsigned were reluctant to become "Replacements."

We realized the best pool of talent was already on hand for spring training—our own minor leaguers. It was a realization that would hit nearly every other team as well.

It was an emotional spring. Tommy Lasorda accepted this strange situation with great enthusiasm, enjoying the opportunity to give instruction and encouragement to the young players.

When we asked our minor leaguers about playing in exhibition games and preparing to play the regular season, we fully recognized the importance of their decision. We advised them to consult with their agents and families and made every effort to present the plan in an objective manner, detailing all possible ramifications of their situation.

They knew they could be labeled "scabs."

On the positive side, the minor leaguers who elected to play in spring games knew they would be coached and evaluated by our major league staff. We also offered the players a salary structure that was an increase for most of them, and a guarantee they would have an opportunity to play in our minor-league system the full year after the strike ended, as it surely would.

Our primary belief was that the players themselves would make the best decisions. In other words, a top prospect who felt he was going to reach the majors anyway wasn't likely to agree to play in the spring games. That was fine with us. In fact, it was what we wanted.

One young player—outfielder Chris Latham—pulled me aside after a meeting with the team and said he had an important question.

Chris asked if I believed he had the ability to play in the big leagues. I told Chris there was no doubt in my mind that he had major league ability. He was a switch-hitting centerfielder with good speed. Chris had stolen 61 bases the previous year while at Bakersfield and Yakima.

When I gave Chris my evaluation, I felt he would turn down the offer to be a replacement player. Much to my surprise, he decided to play.

As our first game of the spring—against the New York Yankees at Ft. Lauderdale—approached, we met with 90 minor leaguers. These young men had one overriding question: "If we play in the spring games, will it ruin our chance of ever being added to the Dodgers' 40-man major league roster?"

It was a serious question, and I gave a serious answer: "The Dodgers always have selected players for the major league roster based on ability. No other factor. As long as I'm the general manager, we will maintain that policy."

I gave my word that spring to a group of young players faced with what might be the most important decision of their baseball careers. I had every intention of keeping my promise.

On March 1, we had commitments from 30 minor leaguers to travel to Ft. Lauderdale. The players had decided to move forward after several gut-wrenching days. None of them had signed replacement-player contracts at the time, operating instead under the standard minor league contract.

If there was an organization that did a better job of providing an objective picture of this unique situation to its players, I didn't hear about it.

"I'm very happy," Tommy told the *Vero Beach Press-Journal.* "I think we're going to have a good ballclub and make the people who come to see us play very interested. If they're looking for a good brand of baseball, we'll give it to them."

At the end of spring training, 35 Dodger replacement players returned to Southern California for the Freeway Series with the Angels. Those 35 had a dream of playing in the big leagues, but realized their chances were slim. For the most part, they were overachievers.

After one game at Anaheim Stadium and another at Dodger Stadium, those dreams appeared to have ended as dramatically as they had begun. At the end of the most unusual exhibition season in baseball history, a judge's ruling in favor of the Players' Association—stating that salary arbitration and free agency were mandatory subjects of collective bargaining—opened the doors for the players to call off their strike.

And that they finally did.

We were headed back to Vero Beach for another session of spring training with our regular players, and our replacement players were off to minor league assignments.

It wasn't to be the end of the story, however.

In late August, we were in a battle for the NL West title when our third baseman, Tim Wallach, went down with an injury to his left knee, forcing us to place him on the 15-day disabled list.

There was no question who was the best replacement for Wallach in our farm system. It was Mike Busch, third baseman for Albuquerque, our Triple A team.

Everybody knew Mike had been a replacement player. Those who were close to me also knew I would keep my word in regard to those players. And I did, bringing up Busch, who was hitting .274 for Albuquerque with 18 homers and 62 RBIs.

On Tuesday, August 29, just after our return from an 11-game road trip and prior to a series opener against the Mets, two players asked to visit with me.

Mike Piazza and Eric Karros came into my office to plead their case on behalf of the team and, I assume, on behalf of the Players' Association. They told me it was a mistake to bring Busch up.

I listened to them patiently, then replied that Busch was the player who could help us the most, and he was here to do just that. I also was hopeful, I said, that Wallach would be able to return to the lineup after 15 days on the disabled list.

Shortly after, I had a telephone call from Karros in the Dodger clubhouse. "Fred, you had better come down here," he said. "You have a lot of unhappy players."

They were assembled in the players' lounge, a room where players relax and eat before and after games. There was nothing relaxing about this meeting, however.

There was only one player missing from the meeting, Mike Busch. I explained to the others that, throughout the history of the Dodgers, players had been called up to the big leagues based on only one thing—ability.

There was no yelling or shouting. The players gave me an opportunity to explain my reasoning. I told the group that Busch was the best candidate in our system to replace Wallach.

I didn't invite Tommy Lasorda or the members of the coaching staff to be in attendance because Busch's promotion had been a management decision, and I didn't want to put Tommy in a position that might cause a rift between him and his players. I must say, Tommy took a very low profile during this period of turmoil.

Having listened to my thoughts, the players expressed their concerns. Pitcher Tom Candiotti, a person I respect a great deal, said it was very hard for him to concentrate on pitching with all of the unrest caused by Busch's arrival.

I told Tom I could appreciate his viewpoint, but he was a major league pitcher, and he and his teammates would just have to deal with the decision.

Veteran outfielder Roberto Kelly, whom I had acquired earlier in the season in a trade with Montreal, spoke out strongly against the move.

It was a discussion I had no plans of prolonging in that I had no intention of changing my decision. I told the players that, if any of them wanted to be the general manager, they could go upstairs and fill out an application for the position, but, until one of them became the GM, I would make the decisions on player personnel.

I wish I would have taken the opportunity to tell them how I felt they should respond to the situation, welcoming Busch as they would any other new teammate, but I'm not sure the players wanted to hear this from me.

Instead, many of the players distanced themselves from Busch during his first game, and the end result was a firestorm at Dodger Stadium, and ultimately in the press. The reaction of the fans was in very loud support of Busch. Ironically, the player who found himself in the middle of the firestorm was our centerfielder, Brett Butler.

Brett's tenure with the Dodgers had already been affected by the strike. He had been our leadoff man for four seasons, but was a free agent at the end of 1994. With the uncertainty created by the strike and due to payroll limitations, we decided to pass on Brett in 1995 and go with younger outfielders. Butler signed as a free agent with the Mets. In early August, however, when we lost outfielder Todd Hollandsworth because of a broken thumb, I made a trade with the Mets to reacquire Brett.

He was welcomed back enthusiastically by both his teammates and Dodger fans, but when he made a few pro-union statements related to the Busch situation, the hearty cheers Butler had been receiving turned into ugly boos.

Dodger fans not only had their say in person, but in the sports sections of their local papers as well.

Within a few days of the Busch decision, 255 people had written to the *Los Angeles Times*. "Of those 255 people who were moved enough to write, 96.5 percent of them thought Butler and the Dodger players were acting like a bunch of four-year-olds sucking their thumbs," wrote *Times* sports editor Bill Dwyre.

"The 255 letters are a startling number. Almost no other sports story here in the last decade or so has drawn that kind of response in that short a time."

Brett told me he would like to have a press conference to smooth over the agitated feelings, a press conference with Busch present.

It was held, with Busch and Butler at the head table. The atmosphere was tense, but ultimately, the media session helped us move forward. And with the issue behind us, our team took flight.

We were in second place with a 64-59 record when our homestand ended on September 6, but we opened our road trip with a three-game sweep in Pittsburgh, Busch delivering two key home runs in that series.

We went on to finish 78-66, good enough to win the division title, and Cincinnati swept us in three games in postseason play.

In reflection, nearly a decade later, was it a mistake to bring Busch up? I can tell you I would make the same move today. The commissioner had told teams to prepare a squad to play regular-season games. Games that would count. If you don't take that assignment seriously, you don't belong in the game. Unfortunately, many teams turned their backs on their replacement players.

There are several players in the big leagues today who served as replacement players for the Dodgers, including pitchers Matt Herges and Eddie Oropesa. They are not recognized as members of the union. They probably never will be.

Mike Busch played in Korea and now is helping other players with big-league dreams as a coach in the independent Northern League. Chris Latham played for three major league teams—Minnesota, Toronto and the New York Yankees—before moving on to Japan. Jay Kirkpatrick, a first baseman who was voted the top player among the Dodger replacements, went on to play in Taiwan and now manages in the Northern League.

I received my share of media criticism for calling Busch up. Baseball writer Ken Daley wrote that, if the Dodgers didn't win their division, the Busch decision would be grounds for firing me. *Sports Illustrated* writer Tom Verducci termed me "naïve." And a few members of the media maintained the Dodgers were trying to break the union.

Nothing could have been further from the truth. We recognized the Players' Association and understood its objectives. Just as the union had a position to uphold, so did the teams.

I don't believe major league baseball will ever again attempt to field a team of replacements.

A lot of young players have had to pay a heavy price because of a labor dispute. They were asked to serve a need at a critical time and they served. I'm proud the Dodger organization stood behind them.

CHAPTER XII

ANATOMY OF A TRADE

N o matter how many trades you make as the general manager of a major league team, you never seem to forget the smallest details of each one.

Of course, if you make what turns out to be a particularly bad trade, it's easy to remember because the media never will let you forget.

I wanted as much good information as possible when I researched a possible trade. I relied heavily on the views of the manager, the coaching staff, scouts and minor league managers and instructors.

Even so, when it came time to make a deal, I realized the total responsibility rested on me, and I accepted that responsibility.

I don't believe a writer covering our team or anyone in baseball ever heard me say, "Well, I made the deal because this person or that person thought it was the right move."

I've heard some general managers reflect on a trade that turned out poorly and defend the action by saying it was a "group decision." There are no group decisions. There is input from the advisers you trust the most, but the buck stops at the door of the GM.

When I had completed a transaction, I felt it to the very core of my existence. It was for this reason that, when Dodger president Bob Graziano called me in May of 1998 to inform me a Mike Piazza trade

Visiting with former AL President Lee MacPhail (seated)
and Yankee executive Gene Michael at Cooperstown, N.Y.

had been consummated without my knowledge, I realized my role as GM would never be the same.

When I was appointed general manager in April of 1987, I accepted the position with the stipulation I would have full and complete responsibility. Peter O'Malley granted me that responsibility and he remained good to his word. Few, if any, general managers had more support from their owners than I had from Peter, and for that, I always will be grateful.

My first significant trade took place a little more than a month after I had replaced Al Campanis as GM.

We had started the 1987 season with a player named Mike Ramsey as our centerfielder. Mike was a converted pitcher who had made the jump from Double A San Antonio. It became obvious very early that the leap from the Texas League to the big leagues was too much for Mike. I was just settling into my chair as GM when I realized I was going to have to act quickly to find another centerfielder.

I didn't have a lot of options with our payroll for the season in place, so I was going to have to make a low-budget deal or swap players where the salaries balanced out.

After a discussion with our scouts, I zeroed in on three centerfielders—John Shelby of the Orioles, Henry Cotto of the Yankees and Joe Orsulak of the Pirates.

Cotto was the only one of the three playing at the major league level at the time. Shelby had been sent to Triple A Rochester, N.Y. after batting .188 for the Orioles. Orsulak had suffered a foot injury and was on a rehabilitation assignment in the Pacific Coast League.

I knew Orsulak from his first four seasons with the Pirates, and I liked his hard-nosed style, but his injury was a concern. As it turned out, Joe never did get healthy enough to play in the big leagues in 1987.

My primary focus turned to Shelby, a switch-hitter who had spent part of seven seasons with the Orioles without a great deal of success. John was a good-looking athlete who seemed to have the necessary tools, but for some reason, things hadn't clicked for him in terms of cracking the starting lineup.

Strangely enough, I had focused on Shelby during an exhibition game in Vero Beach that spring when former Dodger outfielder Lou Johnson was sitting beside me in the press box at Holman Stadium during a game against the Orioles. Johnson had pointed out Shelby because they were both from Lexington, Ky. "Sweet Lou" was telling me what a wonderful man his friend John was. I made a mental note.

My very first trade was a small deal in early May in which I had sent pitcher Balvino Galvez to the Detroit Tigers for catcher Orlando Mercado. Then, on May 21, 1987, I made my first major deal.

Our team had just arrived in New York on the heels of six consecutive losses. The Dodger beat writers were called to my suite at the Grand Hyatt Hotel and I announced the trade—I had sent relief pitcher Tom Niedenfuer to the Orioles for Shelby and pitcher Brad Havens. I had completed the deal that morning with veteran Baltimore GM Hank Peters.

My initial talks with Peters had focused on Niedenfuer for Shelby and outfielder Jim Dwyer, but, because Dwyer had gotten hot, Hank told me he couldn't put the veteran left-handed hitter in the deal.

Nevertheless, I must admit I was excited about this first big trade. I had brought us a player who would be our regular centerfielder and I could hardly wait to call John and tell him the news.

He was at his apartment in Rochester, N.Y. when he received my call. "John, we have just made a trade to acquire you and I want you to report to our team tonight," I said, excitement in my voice.

"Mr. Claire, I can't report tonight," John replied. "My wife and family are with me here in Rochester, and it will take me at least two days to get to Albuquerque."

John was obviously assuming he was going from the Orioles' Triple A team in Rochester to the Dodgers' top farm club.

"John, you aren't going to Albuquerque," I said. "The Dodgers are here in New York and I want you to be in uniform tonight at Shea Stadium. You are the starting centerfielder of the Los Angeles Dodgers."

There was no immediate response from John. It seemed to me the silence must have lasted for a minute or more.

Finally, he replied. "Mr. Claire, I've waited all of my life to hear those words. I will be at Shea Stadium tonight. Thank you very much."

John was on cloud nine and so was I. My wife Sheryl and I celebrated by going to Carnegie Deli for lunch, a spot that became one of our favorites in New York.

John not only became our regular centerfielder, but also one of the top players at that position in 1987. In 120 games for the Dodgers, he batted .277 with 26 doubles, 21 home runs, 69 RBIs and 16 stolen bases. He finished second on our team in home runs and third in RBIs. And he played great defense in center field.

Was it simply a lucky trade? I think it was a result of good scouting. I had sent our veteran pro scout, Mel Didier, into Rochester to follow Shelby in the week before the trade.

Mel loved an assignment where he zeroed in on a guy when we had the chance to make a deal. It was cold in Rochester, and Mel would walk into the park wearing an overcoat with the collar turned up and a big hat to hide his face. This was CIA stuff.

Didier would call me and tell me how impressed he was with Shelby's work habits before the games. "This guy is at the park early, and he goes about his business in a professional way," said Mel.

Most guys sent down to the minors after time in the big leagues have a way of moping around, not realizing there are a number of people in the park making judgments.

After a number of daily conversations with Mel, I wrote a summary of his reports on Shelby: "Excellent person. Good face. Great shape—tall and lean. Not certain good leadoff man. Centerfield best position. Quick arm, charges ball. He didn't break the wrong way one time. Offensively, has trouble with ball down. More power right-handed. Could steal 30 to 40 bases. Alert base runner."

The next season, John was our starting centerfielder on a team that wound up winning the world championship. He batted .263 in 1988 with 23 doubles, 10 home runs, 64 RBIs and 16 stolen bases.

It took a while for National League scouts and pitchers to catch up with John, but they did. He started to see more off-speed pitches and breaking balls. The result: he hit .183 in 1989 and .250 in 1990 for the Dodgers. John spent his final season in the big leagues with Detroit in 1991.

Shelby's statistics may have changed, but his presence and personality never did. He prepared for every game he ever played, ran all-out to first base every time he hit a ground ball and never lost his composure.

He is also a solid family man. He and his wife, Trina, have raised six wonderful children and still reside in Lexington. Lou Johnson's initial report on John was right on target.

We rehired John as a minor league manager in our organization in 1994, and he has served as a major league coach for the Dodgers the past six seasons.

The Shelby acquisition speaks to several points when it comes to the business of making trades. Bottom line—character counts.

The most undervalued part of a player evaluation (with apologies to Billy Beane and "Moneyball") is the makeup of a player. And when you talk about makeup, you had better be talking to your scouts and other personnel who are watching players on a daily basis.

Before my first year as GM was finished in 1987, I made several other deals, some large, some small. Two of those trades proved to be extremely beneficial the following season when we were battling for and won the championship.

In late August, the Oakland A's were looking for a veteran left-hander to help them in the pennant stretch. We had such a player in Rick Honeycutt, a good pitcher who was struggling with a 2-12 record and 4.59 ERA.

I had a number of discussions with Oakland general manager Sandy Alderson, one of the best in the business and a good friend. On August 29, we sent Honeycutt to the A's for young right-handed pitcher Tim Belcher.

From the Dodger standpoint, it was another case of good scouting and the good character of a player coming together to produce a successful deal.

Belcher had been the first selection in the secondary phase of the 1984 draft, but he was just coming into his own in his fourth minor league season when we obtained him.

When you talk about the makeup of a player, people don't come any better than Tim Belcher. We had a good read on his character from our amateur scout in Ohio, Carl Lowenstein.

Belcher was born in the small Ohio town of Sparta. It didn't matter how small it was. There was no town or baseball field in the state that Lowenstein didn't know or hadn't visited. Carl's report, as always, was direct—"Fred, this guy has a great arm and he's an outstanding individual. If we have a chance to get him, I vote yes."

Carl's vote always was good enough for me, and Belcher delivered in a big way. Tim made his first appearance for the Dodgers on September 6, 1987 at Dodger Stadium and pitched two shutout innings for the victory as we snapped a nine-game losing streak by beating the Mets 3-2 in 16 innings. It was a good omen.

When Tim made his first major league start in Cincinnati on September 9, I invited his parents to sit with me at Riverfront Stadium. We lost 4-1, but Belcher won his next three starts to finish the season with a 4-2 record and 2.38 ERA. We had ourselves an outstanding starting pitcher.

Belcher was an important part of our starting rotation in 1988, compiling a record of 12-6 with four complete games and four saves. He struck out 152 batters in 179 2/3 innings with only 51 walks. Belcher also won three games in postseason play. He had arrived.

CHAPTER XIII

TRADING STORIES:
A MULLIGAN AND A MURRAY

My buddy George Green, who used to run KABC radio, believes you are entitled to a mulligan on the first tee. There's one baseball trade where I could have used George's mulligan, where I wish I could have had a second chance.

That trade, of course, was the one that sent Pedro Martinez to the Montreal Expos on November 17, 1993 in exchange for second baseman Delino DeShields.

One thing I want to make clear is that I think the world of Delino. I liked him as a player and I like him as a person. It's not a question of personality. The trade just didn't work out for the Dodgers.

I really didn't want to trade Pedro, whom I respect a great deal. What I wanted to do, as we looked to the 1994 season, was to fill a need at second base, to provide our team with speed along with good defense.

I thought we had filled that need the previous November when I traded for Jody Reed at the expansion draft. That was an interesting transaction in that I had worked out a deal with both expansion teams—the Florida Marlins and Colorado Rockies—to acquire Jody after the veteran infielder was exposed in the draft by the Red Sox.

If Florida selected Reed before Colorado, we had agreed to send outfielder Henry Rodriguez to the Marlins. When the Rockies made the first move to acquire Reed, we were ready with another player they had previously agreed to, pitcher Rudy Seanez.

Ironically, I was talking with Boston general manager Lou Gorman and Mets GM Al Harizin before the draft when Al asked Lou if he thought he would lose any regulars. "I don't believe so," replied Lou. I just smiled, knowing that if things went according to plan, we were going to land Jody Reed.

Reed delivered just what we were looking for in 1993, hitting .276 in 132 games and making only five errors. Jody's hustling style won our fans over in one season.

I wanted very much to sign Jody at the end of that season, making it our first order of business. Shortly after the final out of our season, we made an offer to Jody and his agent, J.D. Dowell—a three-year deal worth $7.8 million ($800,000 signing bonus, $2 million in 1994 and $2.5 million in each of the following two seasons).

I told J.D. the offer would be on the table until the period when Jody could file for free agency, which was the day after the World Series ended.

I stressed to J.D. that we had made our best and only offer right from the beginning. That would give Jody plenty of time to consider it. And if Jody elected instead to test free agency, it would give us time to pursue other candidates for second base. We wouldn't do that without taking the offer off the table.

Sure enough, Jody filed for free agency and our offer was removed. I couldn't understand Jody's failure to accept our proposal in that I had examined the market for second basemen and knew we were being more than fair.

I pressed J.D. to take the deal, but his counter proposal was $11.25 million for three years. I told him I thought he was making a major mistake.

I was frustrated by the fact our offer wasn't accepted, but I turned to other options, talking to the agents of Harold Reynolds and Robby Thompson.

Reynolds had played the 1993 season at Baltimore after 10 years with the Seattle Mariners. Harold is a classy guy, but he was 33 and not a long-term fit for us.

Thompson was coming off his eighth and best season as the San Francisco second baseman. Robby had hit .312 in 1993 with 30 doubles, 19 homers and 65 RBIs.

Thompson was a tough, smart player who would have been a great fit. And what could be better than taking away a key player from the Giants?

We had serious conversations with Robby's agent, Jim Hammonds, but we never made an offer. Hammonds felt Robby would have to be overwhelmed with something in the area of $16 million over four years, but still had reservations about Robby breaking ties with the Giants.

The Giants apparently felt the heat of our interest because they signed Robby to a three-year deal at $11.6 million. The signing had other ramifications for San Francisco. Giant first baseman Will Clark signed a five-year deal with Texas a short time later.

With the Thompson signing, J.D. called me to say that the Giants had "set the market for second basemen." I told J.D. that wasn't our market.

With Thompson signed and Reed's agent stuck in an area that was unacceptable to us, I again looked elsewhere for a second baseman.

I had engaged in talks with Montreal general manager Dan Duquette at the GM meetings and learned DeShields was available for a price. That price was Pedro, and that was the reason I had turned my attention elsewhere.

In four full seasons with the Expos, DeShields, still just 24, had hit .277 and averaged more than 46 stolen bases a season. He was the leader of a youthful Expo team and generally regarded as one of the best young second basemen in the game.

I made two calls before moving forward with the deal—one to Tommy Lasorda and one to Ralph Avila, the man in charge of our baseball operations in the Dominican Republic. I told both men they had veto rights on the trade. Both agreed it was a good deal for the Dodgers in that we would solve our problem at second with an outstanding young player.

The deal was made. There are no mulligans in baseball.

If Jody accepts our offer, we keep Pedro Martinez. If we sign Robby Thompson, we keep Pedro, and Will Clark probably stays with the Giants. Ifs don't matter in baseball.

Jody Reed signed a contract for the 1994 season with the Milwaukee Brewers for $750,000.

I think the deals I'm most proud of are those that brought us John Shelby, Tim Belcher, Alfredo Griffin, Jay Howell, Jesse Orosco and John Tudor, because those moves had a connection with our World Series victory in 1988. After all, there's only one real goal in any season, and that's to win a world championship.

Another move I feel good about was the addition of Eddie Murray, a man who entered the Hall of Fame in the summer of 2003. The trade for Murray actually had its start when our team was staying in San Francisco during the '88 World Series. I had several meetings with Baltimore general manager Roland Hemond, for whom Murray was then playing.

Roland seemed amazed I would be willing to talk about a trade while our team was in the World Series, but I felt if we could land Eddie we might be making a return trip to the Fall Classic.

Eddie had enjoyed a dozen highly successful seasons in Baltimore, but he reportedly had become disenchanted because of comments made by the Orioles' ownership.

It wasn't going to be an easy deal in that Eddie had a long-term contract that still had three years remaining at $2.3 million per season. It was a big financial obligation at the time, but Peter O'Malley (after saying emphatically, "He makes how much?" when I told him the figures) gave me the approval to move ahead with a deal.

My talks with Roland carried through the World Series, into the GM meetings in Scottsdale, Ariz., and eventually into a meeting in a Chicago airport hotel.

The deal for Eddie was finally completed at the winter meetings in Atlanta on December 4, 1988.

But first, there was a last-minute holdup.

Literally.

After completing the final details of the transaction in my hotel suite, I, several other representatives of our club, and several Oriole executives entered a glass elevator and headed to the floor where the press room was located.

As we neared our destination, and with the members of the media looking on, the elevator came to a sudden stop between floors. It seemed amusing at first, but as the glass started to fog up, the light-hearted banter fell silent.

"This is going to make a heck of a story," said Roland.

"I just hope we get a chance to read it," chimed in Oriole scout and longtime baseball man Birdie Tebbets.

The deal—when finally announced after face-to-face meetings in San Francisco, Scottsdale, Chicago, Atlanta, and one long elevator ride—brought Eddie Murray home to Los Angeles, where he was born and raised, in exchange for shortstop Juan Bell and pitchers Brian Holton and Ken Howell.

If my old friend George Green was going to give a second mulligan, I would use it on the trade in which we acquired outfielder Eric Davis from Cincinnati for pitchers Tim Belcher and John Wetteland.

In many ways, this was much like the Martinez-DeShields deal in that we were trying to fill a specific need and ended up overpaying.

The trade for Davis came on November 27, 1991. A year earlier, we had signed outfielder Darryl Strawberry as a free agent. Here were two great baseball talents in what should have been the prime of their careers, reunited as Dodgers close to their roots in South Central Los Angeles.

Eric Davis, 29 at the time of the trade, played two injury-plagued seasons for us. He wasn't able to provide the power we were looking for and soon was a source of frustration for Tommy Lasorda, who had pushed very hard for the deal.

A spring or two after Davis' tenure as a Dodger, I was sitting at a spring training game with veteran baseball man Joe Klein. "Fred," he told me, "when you signed Strawberry and traded for Eric Davis, I said to myself, 'They are going to fly another world championship banner at Dodger Stadium.'"

That's exactly what I envisioned when we brought Eric and Darryl back to Los Angeles.

It didn't happen that way. Baseball can break your heart if you let it.

CHAPTER XIV

BASEBALL FREE AGENTS... ANYTHING BUT FREE

The first true free agent of modern times was a Dodger, pitcher Andy Messersmith. It wasn't a role he sought. He didn't set out to boldly go where no player had gone before. He didn't even want to become a free agent. He wanted to stay with the Dodgers. And he wanted to ensure that would happen by getting a no-trade clause in his contract. That's all he wanted.

I remember well the trade by Al Campanis that brought Andy to our club. I was attending the winter meetings for the fourth time as a member of the Dodger organization in late November of 1972. This figured to be one of the most enjoyable of those gatherings since the meetings were being held at the Royal Hawaiian Hotel in Honolulu.

I received a call from Campanis late on the evening of November 28 to come to his room. There was a press announcement to be made.

Al had just completed a major deal with the Angels, acquiring Messersmith and third baseman Ken McMullen for five players—pitchers Bill Singer and Mike Strahler, outfielders Frank Robinson and Bobby Valentine, and infielder Billy Grabarkewitz.

The deal proved to be one of Campanis' very best. Messersmith responded with three outstanding seasons for the Dodgers, winning

Fred and Dodger pitcher Andy Messersmith.

14 games in 1973, 20 in 1974 as he helped pitch our club into the World Series for the first time in eight years, and 19 in 1975.

After his 20-victory season, Andy wanted to be assured he wouldn't be traded. He loved everything about Southern California.

Blessed with boyish good looks, Andy always appeared to have just stepped off a surfboard. He had a great personality and a relaxed attitude. If there was a guy made for the cool Southern California scene, it was Andy.

When his day to pitch rolled around, however, look out. He was so focused that, when he walked into the clubhouse, it was as though he was wearing blinders. He didn't smile, didn't even say hello. He was, as they say, in a zone.

Very frankly, Andy was my kind of pitcher. Some members of our organization were turned off by his tunnel vision on game day. I chalked it up to his great competitive spirit. For whatever reasons, Andy and I developed what I have always considered to be a very good relationship.

Andy's relationship with Campanis turned in a different direction. It was Al's job to sign Messersmith to a contract for the 1975 season and Andy was determined not to sign unless he had the no-trade stipulation.

No-trade contracts weren't part of the package for major league teams at that point, and Al was determined to hold the line on behalf of the Dodgers. So he went ahead and renewed Andy's contract for the '75 season.

Under the rules of the day, a club could utilize the reserve clause contained in every contract to renew that contract at the same salary season after season, if it so chose, without even requiring the player's signature. Players remained the property of the club that originally signed them unless they were traded or released. The owners labeled free agency a radical idea that could doom baseball.

At one point, Andy came to me and said he would agree to sign for 1975 with one stipulation. Peter O'Malley would have to give his word Andy wouldn't be traded.

Peter discussed Andy's proposal with John Gaherin, baseball's chief negotiator at the time, and was told it wouldn't be a good idea to make such a verbal commitment to a player.

Ironically, Peter had his own concerns about the reserve clause. As a student at the University of Pennsylvania, Peter had been in a class in which the language of the baseball contracts had been discussed. The professor of the class, Peter told me, felt the reserve clause represented a potential problem for ownership.

The professor was right.

Both Messersmith and Montreal pitcher Dave McNally played in 1975 under renewed contracts, although McNally retired in June.

Marvin Miller and the Major League Baseball Players' Association maintained the two players were no longer under contract to their teams after the season and should be declared free agents.

The union filed grievances on behalf of both. On December 23, 1975, arbitrator Peter Seitz ruled in favor of the players, striking down baseball's ages-old reserve system. The owners, who had hired Seitz, fired him and appealed the decision, but it was upheld.

Atlanta Braves owner Ted Turner ultimately signed Messersmith for $1.75 million after a bidding war. Andy encountered shoulder problems and was 16-15 in two years with the Braves, then 0-3 for the New York Yankees in 1978. Messersmith returned to the Dodgers in 1979, going 2-4 in 11 starts before being released in August of that season. I must admit I had encouraged Campanis to bring Andy back.

Unfortunately for Andy, he never was the same pitcher after the 1975 season. And baseball never would be the same with the advent of free agency.

The Dodgers managed to stay away from the bidding wars for free agents until after the 1979 season. We had been in the World Series in 1977 and 1978 against the Yankees, but fell to third place with a 79-83 record in 1979, $11^{1}/2$ games out.

It was at that point that Peter felt it was time for the tradition-rich Dodgers to enter the brave new world of free agency.

In a strange twist for Peter, he decided to become the point man in that brave new world. He asked Campanis what he felt our team needed to improve in 1980 and which free agents out there could bring about that improvement.

Al said the need was pitching, so we went after both a starter and reliever with Peter leading the way in the negotiations. In November, we signed starter Dave Goltz to a six-year deal for $3 million, and followed that by landing reliever Don Stanhouse for five years at a cost of $2.1 million.

I'll never forget a call we had with Stanhouse after he had been signed. Don was on a speaker phone, and both Al and I were in Peter's office.

"What do you think of Dave Goltz, who we have also just signed?" Peter asked Stanhouse, apparently looking for some reassurance.

"Now that you have me, you should be OK," said the relief pitcher.

As it turned out, we weren't OK with either Goltz or Stanhouse. Goltz was gone after two-plus seasons with a 9-19 record, and Stanhouse lasted just one year in which he went 2-2 with a 5.04 ERA.

After that experience, we backed off the free-agent market for several years, but when I was appointed GM, Peter gave me approval to try again.

I would have to say the two most visible free-agent signings I was involved with produced mixed results. I refer to the signing of Kirk Gibson prior to the 1988 season and Darryl Strawberry prior to 1991.

Kirk, of course, delivered a great season in 1988 and was the driving force of our world championship team. Things didn't go as well the following two seasons for him because he was limited by injuries, but there never was a time that he failed to give us the best of what he had to give.

Kirk and I got along very well with one notable exception—a rather loud shouting match in Tommy Lasorda's office at Dodger Stadium on the Sunday prior to the All-Star Game in 1990.

Kirk had decided it was time to move on. His hope was to be traded to a team close to his home in Michigan, and he had made this request to me.

I told Kirk we would do our best to accommodate him, but my first obligation was to our team, and I wasn't going to make a deal unless I felt it benefited the Dodgers.

Kirk said he understood, but his patience was wearing thin. Finally, anxious over what he perceived as a lack of effort on my part, he asked to meet with me prior to our home game with Pittsburgh on Sunday, July 8. I told him I would meet him in Tommy's office.

I knew Kirk had the reputation of always getting what he wanted, but I didn't quite anticipate his approach in our pregame meeting. With Tommy sitting behind his desk, Kirk and I chose to stand for our discussion.

It didn't take long before the words became a little heated, and then he touched off a rocket with me by declaring: "You're not doing your job. You need to trade me."

My immediate reaction was to shout back: "You're not going to tell me how to do my job."

Kirk responded with something along the lines of, "Have you ever seen a big bear in the woods?"

I moved my sunglasses to the top of my head and fired back, "No, do you know of any?"

It was now an all-out shouting match as we went nose to nose, and Tommy pleaded, "Fellows, please quiet down."

I'm not sure what I was doing in a heated discussion with Kirk Gibson in that the only way I could match up would be the volume of my voice. As it turned out, our voices were loud enough (I was told later) to be heard throughout the Dodger clubhouse. I departed for the All-Star Game and then called Kirk the next day at his home in Michigan.

"It's a good thing you have a mild-mannered agent in Doug Baldwin to help you, because you have a hell of a temper," I told him.

"Fred, don't tell me about my temper," Kirk replied. "When you put your glasses on the top of your head and start yelling at me, I don't want to hear about *my* temper."

It turned out to be a good conversation, and we agreed to meet before our game with the Cubs at Wrigley Field the first day back after the All-Star break.

There was a strange sense of calm as Kirk and I found a spot in a room off the visiting clubhouse to continue our discussion.

"Kirk, the only way I can trade you is that if it's a deal that helps the Dodgers," I told him, repeating what I had been saying from the start.

"I understand, Fred," Kirk replied. "I know you have a job to do, and I will do everything I can to help this team as long as I'm here."

We were 12 games out at the All-Star break with a 39-42 record. Kirk came charging back in the second half, and we finished 10 games over .500 at 86-76, good enough for second place.

After finishing the season with us, Kirk became a free agent. I subsequently received a call from Herk Robinson, the general manager of the Kansas City Royals, asking my thoughts about Gibson.

"If you have a chance to sign Kirk, I would sign him," I told Robinson. "He can help your team. He can help any team he's with. He's a winner."

Kirk signed with the Royals, and two years later, returned to the Detroit Tigers.

Kirk is now a coach for the Tigers and, one day soon, he will be a big-league manager. I'm going to enjoy watching his teams play, just as I enjoyed watching him play.

No free agent had more talent than Darryl Strawberry. But there are no championship stories to be written about Darryl as a Dodger.

The strangest twist to the Strawberry signing is that a no-trade clause, the very provision that opened the door for Andy Messersmith, was a factor in signing Darryl to a Dodger contract.

You might consider this a reach, but the free agent I wanted to sign after the 1989 season was Montreal Expo pitcher Mark Langston. On the evening of December 1, 1989, club attorney Sam Fernandez and I were in the office of agent Arn Tellem, seemingly on the verge of signing Langston.

We had worked out most of the deal, the only thing holding us up being our firm stand on a total no-trade stipulation. I felt Mark would be a perfect fit for us, and we were willing to give some ground in the no-trade discussion when Tellem said he needed to make a call.

Arn came back into the room with a stunning announcement: "Mark Langston has just signed a five-year deal with the Angels."

Sam and I closed our briefcases and slumped out of the room.

Tellem called the next morning, somewhat apologetic, and said he knew coming to Southern California was important for Mark and his wife, Michelle, but they made the decision to sign with the Angels because the club offered a no-trade clause.

If we had signed Langston, it's clear there wouldn't have been room in the budget to sign Darryl one year later. That being said, when we gave Darryl a five-year deal in November of 1990, he was coming off a season in which he had hit 37 home runs and driven in 107. He was 28 years old, a veteran of eight seasons in the big leagues and on pace to become one of the great power hitters in baseball history.

It was a homecoming for Darryl, who had graduated from Crenshaw High School, but after one good year, being home proved to be no haven from his problems. Darryl hit 28 home runs and drove in 99 in 1991, but he played in only 75 games the next two years because of injuries and off-the-field difficulties. We kept trying to keep Darryl on the right path, but there seemed to be too many distractions.

It came to the breaking point at our final exhibition game at Anaheim Stadium in April of 1994. Darryl failed to show up for our Sunday game.

I told the inquiring news media that Darryl didn't have permission to be absent. I told the media I didn't know where Darryl was. It was obvious I was upset. The only feeling greater than my anger was my concern about Darryl's whereabouts. Finally that evening, I received a call from Darryl. "Fred," he said, "I just want you to know I'm OK, and I will be with the team tomorrow."

"No, Darryl, you won't be with the team," I replied. "I want to meet with you tomorrow morning because we have come to the end of the road. You have failed to show the responsibility that is needed to be a part of our team. You can bring any representatives you care to have with you."

We agreed to meet at a law office in downtown Los Angeles. When Darryl walked into that office, he was accompanied by his wife, Charisse, and an attorney I was meeting for the first time, Robert Shapiro, later to gain worldwide fame, of course, in the O.J. Simpson case.

Shapiro got right to the point.

"We want you to know," he said, "that Darryl has a problem with substance abuse. We have talked to the Players' Association about getting assistance for Darryl."

It was hardly a surprise, and I was pleased Darryl was finally going to face one of the problems that had plagued him. He had tears streaming down his face as he embraced me after the meeting. "Fred, I feel so sorry that I have let you and the Dodgers down," he said.

I told Darryl I wanted him to get well, that the most important thing was for him to take care of himself. On April 8, he entered the Betty Ford Clinic. There were other off-the-field problems for Darryl as well, including time in prison.

I lost my temper with him on a number of occasions, usually when he failed to keep a medical appointment. He never once responded with anger. Darryl knew I cared about him. I still do.

Nevertheless, we gave him his release on May 25, and he signed with the San Francisco Giants less than a month later. Darryl was to later return to New York to play his final five seasons, from 1995 through 1999, with the Yankees.

In 1998, after I was fired by the Dodgers, I walked into the Yankee clubhouse at Boston's Fenway Park as a member of the ESPN radio team. I had been assigned to do a couple of interviews prior to the game.

One of the first people I spotted was Darryl, who walked over to give me a warm greeting. Somehow, he had managed to keep his career going. It was a testimony to his talent and his determination.

I was pleased to see Darryl in a big-league uniform. Quite honestly, I was happy to see Darryl Strawberry alive.

CHAPTER XV

THE DEATH AND LIFE OF MAURY WILLS

M aury Wills is dead.

I shuddered when those chilling words echoed through the Dodger Stadium press box that night in 1983. There was a mind-numbing rumor being checked out that Maury had passed away due to a drug overdose.

As shock evolved into deep sadness, I kept asking myself, "Why didn't his friends do more to help?"

And then, a better question: "Why hadn't I done more?"

I got my chance when it turned out to be a false rumor. But an understandable one. There was no question Maury suffered from a serious drug problem.

He had been on a natural high for a long time. At age 26, Maury Wills was still in the minor leagues, his dream of making it to the majors apparently just that, a fanciful dream.

But that year, 1959, he got called up to the Dodgers and proved he not only belonged in the big leagues, but he belonged among the trend-setters at that level. A great leadoff man and a smooth-fielding shortstop, Maury went on to revolutionize the game by bringing back a lost art: Base stealing.

The year before Maury's arrival, Willie Mays led the majors in stolen bases with 31. In 1962, Maury smashed Ty Cobb's single-season stolen base record of 96 by getting 104.

When his playing days, including two stints with the Dodgers, ended, Maury came up with a new dream: To manage in the big leagues. He got that chance as well, with the Seattle Mariners midway through the 1980 season.

But that dream became a nightmare in less than a full season, Maury getting fired midway through his second year with the club. It was a devastating blow, and it sent him into a downhill spiral.

At the bottom, he found drugs. Maury had already been introduced into the dark world of cocaine the previous winter. Once his managerial responsibilities were stripped away, Maury became completely lost in that hazy world.

I was determined to help him find his way back. The day after the death rumor, I called Don Newcombe, a former star pitcher for us who was now a member of our community relations staff and involved in our Employee Assistance Program.

Moreover, Don could relate to Maury's struggle, since he himself had developed an alcohol problem after finding a huge void when his own career ended. Don had returned to sobriety, and I hoped he could help Maury do the same.

Maury lived in Los Angeles, out by the ocean in Marina del Ray. I told Don we needed to go over to Maury's house, confront him and drag him, if necessary, to a rehabilitation clinic.

"Fred," Don cautioned me, "that house is all but boarded up, and he has a couple of big dogs who aren't very friendly when visitors come around."

Nevertheless, with the memory of my guilt over Maury's rumored death still fresh, I was determined.

"Don," I said, "we are going over there tonight to get him."

It wasn't so easy to talk tough when we arrived at the house, dark and seemingly deserted. The lights of nearby boats reflected off the water, providing us with an eerie, flickering illumination of our surroundings. The front door was locked and, worse still, the sound of our knocking started those menacing dogs barking.

We slipped around the side, pushed a gate and it creaked open. As we moved forward cautiously, the barking didn't get any louder. Relieved, we discovered the dogs were locked behind a fence.

We tried a side door and it opened. Inside, with all the lights off, Maury was sitting on a couch, staring into space.

He blankly acknowledged our presence. We told him we knew he had a drug problem, and he didn't protest. We said it was time for him to get professional help, and he didn't argue. He didn't go with us, saying he wasn't ready. But at least, our visit had put the idea of rehabilitation into his head as a real option.

I promised to call Maury and did so on several occasions. Finally, when I told him we might be able to give him a coaching position with the Dodgers if he went to a rehab clinic and stuck with the program, he said he was ready to submit to treatment if I would give him three days to prepare.

He later told me that, had I insisted on coming that day, he wouldn't have been receptive. But in his state of mind, three days seemed like the distant future. I told him Don and I would be at his house on the designated day at 4 p.m. to pick him up.

But when we got there and knocked, there was no answer. Since this was before the era of cell phones, we simply went back to our cars, parked in front of the house, and waited.

What I later learned was that Maury, panicking at the thought of admitting his drug use to others, was crouched behind the blanket that covered his front window, unable to bring himself to open the front door. We waited and waited and finally, after about 20 minutes, that door swung open.

"Why are you waiting out there?" said Maury, acting as if he had just discovered our presence.

"Why didn't you tell me you were here?"

*Former Dodger pitching great Don Newcombe and Fred went to
Maury Wills' home to take him to the Orange County Care Unit.*

He invited us in and said he had to run upstairs to throw a few
things together, as if this was the first time he had even thought about
going to a rehab clinic.

Again we waited about 20 minutes while Maury sat upstairs.
The man who had looked major-league pitchers in the eye hundreds
of times from his perch a few feet off the bag and then taken off,
without fear of failure, on his way to yet another stolen base, was now
trying to summon enough courage to take the few steps required to
get downstairs, the first tentative steps on his journey to recovery.

Finally he took those steps, came down, said to us, "Let's go,"
and off we went, Maury in my 280Z, and Don following behind in
his car.

We took Maury to the Orange County Care Unit and checked him in. He was handed a form with a space for his name at the top. Maury paused for a moment and then wrote in "Donald Claire."

After about a week, Maury was asked to participate in a group session. Each person was to stand up and give his name and a little background information. Maury, once a public figure and a polished speaker, was nervous.

"I have a confession," he told the group. "My name isn't Donald Claire."

In unison, they answered, "Yes, we know, MAURY!"

Maury spent 25 days in the care unit, but, unfortunately, that wasn't the end of the story.

The following spring, I invited him to Vero Beach to serve as a coach and he accepted. Maury did a great job, but, soon thereafter, regressed, succumbing again to his addiction.

Or, as he put it, "The obsession hit me again."

Maury later said he came to realize that he had tried rehabilitation "for all the wrong reasons," because he didn't want to disappoint me. He finally understood he would only be successful when he wanted to do it for himself.

That time came on August 13, 1989. He became sober that day and has been so ever since. The man whose quick bursts of speed had propelled him into baseball history had begun a marathon he knows will last a lifetime.

Several years later, with Maury back with the Dodgers in a coaching capacity, I was taking my afternoon jog around the golf course at Dodgertown when I saw Maury measuring a putt.

A smile crossed my face as I ran by. I had only a small part in Maury's recovery, but I find it difficult to describe the satisfaction that small part gives me to this day.

CHAPTER XVI

NOTHING TO PROVE,
EVERYTHING TO LIVE FOR

When Tommy Lasorda was introduced as the new Dodger manager at Walt Alston's farewell press conference, he was asked if he hoped to manage 23 years as did his predecessor.

Replied Tommy, "I just want to live that long."

It was a remark that evoked laughter in 1976. The subject of life span was no laughing matter for Tommy in 1996. In his 20th season of a Hall of Fame managing career, Tommy, at the age of 68, was experiencing chest pains.

Ultimately that led to an angioplasty procedure on June 26. And ultimately, that led to a decision about Tommy's future.

By 1996, there was nothing more for Tommy to accomplish, nothing more required to assure his entry into Cooperstown. In his two decades as manager, the Dodgers won eight division titles, four pennants and two world championships. With a career record of 1,599-1,439, he ranks 13th on the all-time list in victories and 12th with 3,038 games managed.

Peter and I held several meetings with Tommy after the angioplasty as he pondered whether or not to put his uniform back on and return to the dugout. It was tough for him. Remember, Tommy had worn a baseball uniform in some capacity for most of his life and had loved every minute of it.

Both Peter and I stressed to Tommy the most important thing to him and his family should be his health. I told Tommy that, if he were my brother, I would be telling him the same thing.

After both Peter and I had held several meetings with Tommy, all of us met at Dodger Stadium on a Sunday morning, July 28. It was a quiet Sunday at Dodger Stadium, the team concluding a road trip in Houston. Tommy walked into Peter's office with his wife, Jo.

Peter made it very clear the decision to return was totally in Tommy's hands.

I still remember Peter's words: "Tommy, if you want to continue to manage, you can go down to the clubhouse and put on your uniform and manage. It's up to you."

Tommy's decision: Retirement.

He obviously had given a lot of thought to this very emotional subject. He stated his desire, however, in a very matter-of-fact manner. Tommy believed it was best for him and his family to step aside as manager and remove himself from the stress of the position. He seemed comfortable with the decision. That pleased me.

Quite frankly, though, it also surprised me. And, I was relieved to the extent that, if Tommy had returned as manager and had subsequently suffered a heart attack, I would have felt responsible for being part of the decision-making process that resulted in placing him in a stress-inducing position.

There are those who have implied, or flat out declared, that Tommy was forced out. That simply isn't true. It was Tommy's decision, and my sense of the situation was that he had arrived at his conclusion after a great deal of thought and discussion with his family.

We planned to make the announcement of Tommy's retirement the following day, but instead, the story already was in the morning edition of the *Los Angeles Times*, an exclusive written by columnist Allan Malamud.

Malamud proudly told his closest friend, publicist Bill Caplan, that Lasorda had placed a call from his car as he left Dodger Stadium to inform Malamud of his decision.

"I haven't forgotten that you recommended me for this job and I'm not calling anybody else," Lasorda told Malamud, according to Caplan.

After Malamud wrote in the *Herald-Examiner* in 1976 that it was time for Walt Alston to go, he had followed that up with a column suggesting Tommy should take Walt's place, while Walter and Peter O'Malley had reached the same decision independently. Tommy always felt Malamud had given him a helpful push.

Malamud told Caplan the Lasorda retirement story was "the biggest scoop I've ever had."

Malamud had his scoop because Tommy was concerned enough about his heart to change his lifestyle. Unfortunately, Malamud did not change his lifestyle and, less than two months later, he died of a heart attack.

Tommy at least had the satisfaction of knowing he had rewarded Malamud's support with a career achievement before Allan's time ran out.

CHAPTER XVII

LASORDA TO RUSSELL: A PAINFUL TRANSITION

For the second time in my tenure with the Dodgers, the team was faced with the prodigious task of replacing a giant. In 1976, when Walt Alston's managerial reign ended after 23 seasons, Tommy Lasorda had proved an ideal replacement, lasting 20 years. Now it was again time to choose a field manager, hopefully one who could match Alston and Lasorda in terms of longevity and excellence.

Peter O'Malley and I made what I considered the logical choice. We picked Bill Russell, who had been Tommy's choice to run the club when Tommy was first hospitalized with heart problems.

I felt we should give Bill a contract for the remainder of that 1996 season and 1997, but Peter wanted to add an additional year, and I didn't object. I have always had great respect for Bill, but I also felt short-term contracts for managers had served the Dodgers very well through the years.

I had known Bill since he was an 18-year-old minor league outfielder from Pittsburg, Kan. I remember the struggle he had when he was switched from the outfield to shortstop early in his career. The fans and the media were getting on him quite forcefully.

Bill Russell, Sheryl and Fred at a St. Patrick's
Day party at Dodgertown in Vero Beach, Fla.

And it got to him. He admitted that one day while standing with me and relief pitcher Jim Brewer near our dugout at Dodger Stadium.

"I'm tired of all the bullshit I'm taking from the writers," Bill said. "I'm going to stop talking to those guys."

Jim was from Broken Arrow, Oklahoma, so he and Bill, with common country roots, spoke the same language: Few words, basic values, blunt honesty. And Jim was certainly blunt and honest that day.

"Let me tell you something, Bill," Brewer said, "if you're going to let that shit bother you, go in the clubhouse, take off your uniform and go home."

Bill, of course, did nothing of the sort. Jim's two-sentence pep talk inspired him to stand up to his critics, and he went on to become an all-star and the dean of the Dodgers, playing in a Los Angeles-record 2,181 games. Only Zack Wheat, an outfielder in the Brooklyn days, played more games in Dodger blue.

Bill went on to be a minor-league manager and was in his eighth season as a Dodger coach when we tabbed him to take over in the dugout.

The advice from Brewer, who was later killed in an automobile accident, stuck with Bill through all of the years he was in uniform. There were a lot of things he didn't let bother him. But there were also some things he couldn't shrug off when he became Dodger manager.

Peter and I both knew it wasn't going to be easy for Tommy to step aside, but we felt if anyone had a chance to make the transition easier, it was Bill. It was Tommy who first managed Bill at Ogden, Utah in the Pioneer League in 1966, Tommy who had always been a big supporter of Bill throughout Russell's playing career, and Tommy who had brought him back as a coach. Tommy said more than once that Bill was like his second son.

But when Bill became Tommy's successor, their relationship soured. Bill felt Tommy was second-guessing him. Bill had heard stories from sportswriters about Tommy sitting in the press box, contrasting a move Russell had made with what he would have done.

And, perhaps, Bill felt he needed to distance himself from Tommy's towering presence in order to establish his own identity. After all, Tommy had been given the freedom to establish his own presence when he replaced Alston.

When Tommy occupied the manager's office, the walls were filled with pictures of celebrities. When Bill took over, those pictures were replaced by just one, a picture of John Wayne.

"My personality is not close to Tommy's," Bill said in an *L.A. Times* profile shortly after taking over. "That's just not me. I just can't do that."

Tommy was hurt by Russell's independence. He has confided to friends he couldn't understand Bill's failure to consult him, failure to include him in big decisions, failure to ever ask Tommy, renowned as a motivator, to address the team.

Unfortunately, the alienation between the two men became public in a national spotlight. It was the summer of 1997 and Tommy, then serving the Dodgers as a vice-president and goodwill ambassador, was in Cooperstown for his induction into the Hall of Fame.

Tommy spoke eloquently about the induction and, if he had stuck to that subject, he would have been fine. But, in a Cooperstown press conference, he was asked, if he was a general manager and could have any of the active major league managers to run his team, who would he select?

"This answer might surprise you," Lasorda replied, "but I would take [the New York Mets'] Bobby Valentine."

"Surprise *us?*" wrote *L.A. Times* columnist Bill Plaschke. "One imagines that statement might also surprise Bill Russell, current Dodger manager."

The answer surprised and disappointed me. I was furious. Tommy had once managed Valentine and still felt close to him. But that didn't excuse the remark. Here was the most visible member of our organization talking about his choice for a manager and mentioning someone under contract to another team.

Another remark from Tommy in that press conference: "I've always said, if I can no longer manage, I'd like to be a general manager. But I don't want anybody's job."

It should have been a day of celebration for Tommy. Instead, it became a day of controversy. The headline in the *L.A. Times* the next day read, "To Hall and Back? At 69, Lasorda not yet ready to rest on laurels, but in a perfect world, he might be Dodger general manager, hiring Valentine as manager."

I called Tommy to express my feelings. I told him our organization could be hit with a $250,000 fine by the commissioner's office for tampering by mentioning Valentine.

"Suppose you are managing the Dodgers," I told him, "and suppose our farm director is asked this question: 'If you were a general manager with another team, who would you want as your manager?' And suppose that executive would have replied, 'This answer might surprise you, but I would take Jim Leyland.' How would you have felt?"

Tommy, to his credit, said he recognized he had mishandled his answer. He even offered to resign.

"Tommy, I don't want you to resign," I said. "I just want us to be going in the same direction."

Despite his admission of poor judgment, I wasn't about to condone what Tommy had done publicly. When I was asked by a *Times* reporter the next day if somebody should speak to Tommy about watching his tongue, I said, on the record, "I think that would be appropriate, yes."

Making the adjustment from manager to a front-office role wasn't easy for Tommy. He loved being the manager. In my view, no matter who would have replaced him, it would have been tough for Tommy to watch from a distance.

As it turned out, Bill had a much bigger concern than Tommy. Fox purchased the Dodgers in 1998 and then instigated the shocking trade that sent Mike Piazza to the Florida Marlins. Several days after the blockbuster deal, team president Bob Graziano asked me to think about a replacement for Russell.

When the new Fox ownership pressed Fred to consider a replacement for Manager Bill Russell, his recommendation was Dodger coach Reggie Smith (right), shown here with Hall of Famer Reggie Jackson.

I told Bob, replacing Russell at that point made no sense to me. We had just been through a trade that had turned our team upside down, and I felt we needed time to let things settle down.

Graziano, however, kept pressing the point, and I finally gave him my recommendation. I felt we had two legitimate candidates — bench coach Mike Scioscia and hitting coach Reggie Smith.

There was no question in my mind Scioscia was going to be a successful manager, but I felt our best candidate at that point was Reggie. He was respected by the players and had the strength to take over in a difficult situation.

That was my message to Graziano: If the change was to be made, Reggie Smith should be our next manager.

CHAPTER XVIII

THE SALE TO FOX:
THE O'MALLEYS CROSS
THE EMOTIONAL BARRIER

When Sheryl and I returned home from dinner on Saturday night, January 5, 1997, the red message light on the telephone in my office was flashing. There were two messages awaiting me, both from Peter O'Malley.

In 30 years with the organization, I could never remember Peter leaving TWO messages to return a call.

When I got Peter at his home, he asked if I was free to visit with him at 10 o'clock the next morning at Dodger Stadium.

"Sure," I replied.

"Good, I'll see you then," he said, adding somewhat strangely, "You know how rumors start."

Sheryl was standing nearby as I hung up. "What did Peter want?" she inquired, sensing it must be something of importance.

"Sheryl, Peter is going to sell the team," I responded.

"Did he say that?" she asked.

"No," I said, "but it's the first time I can ever remember that Peter has called me at home to ask me to meet with him without telling me the subject."

Peter had never spoken to me about selling the Dodgers. But I could read him very well after working with him on a daily basis for three decades.

Despite Peter's lack of comment on the subject, I knew he felt it was time to sell. Why? It was an accumulation of events.

When I arrived at the stadium on Sunday morning, the only car in the executive parking section belonged to Peter. I went to my office to await the scheduled meeting and, shortly thereafter, Dodger vice-president Bob Graziano stopped by.

"What do you think this is all about?" Bob asked. I repeated to him what I had told Sheryl.

"I think you're right," Bob concurred.

When Bob and I walked into Peter's office, he was in his normal non-game attire—casual clothes, tennis shoes and a look as relaxed as the clothes he was wearing.

"I've been talking to my family for some time and we've decided to sell the team," said Peter in a manner-of-fact fashion. "We've crossed the emotional barriers, and we know it's time to sell."

It was typical Peter. A major decision had been reached after a great deal of thought and after long discussions with the O'Malley family.

Peter said Bob and I were the first non-family members to know of the decision. He would be meeting with longtime Dodger announcer Vin Scully later in the day. There would be a press conference the following day in the Stadium Club.

Peter was prepared for the task of telling the world through the media that the O'Malleys were selling a family business they had run for nearly half a century. He was calm at the news conference, his words well thought out.

"Family ownership of sports today is a dying breed," Peter declared. "It's a high-risk business. You need a broader base than an individual family to carry you through the storms. Groups or corporations are probably the wave of the future."

From the time Peter announced the team was on the market, he stressed a primary goal—to make the transition after the sale as smooth as possible. The objective was to find quality ownership that subscribed to the basic beliefs that had made the Dodger franchise one of the most respected and valuable in the history of sports.

The very day of the press conference, I told Peter we had a couple of pressing issues on the table: the contracts of catcher Mike Piazza and first baseman Eric Karros. Both players were eligible for arbitration. Karros could be a free agent after the 1997 season and Piazza the following year.

Peter instructed me to deal with the contracts in the fashion I felt best served the team. He expressed reservations about our ability to sign Piazza to a long-term deal in view of the recent signing of Albert Belle (five years for $55 million) by the Chicago White Sox.

As it developed, in January of 1997, we were able to sign Karros to a four-year contract for $20 million and Piazza to a two-year deal for $15 million. The previous month, Peter had given the OK to sign free-agent third baseman Todd Zeile to a three-year deal for $9.5 million. Even though the team was for sale, Peter wasn't going to short-change the players or the fans.

A lot of Monday morning quarterbacks like to look back at the Piazza negotiations of that time and make the case that the Dodgers should have done an Albert Belle-type signing to lock up Mike for the future.

If you put yourself in Peter's position, that type of contract for Piazza didn't make much sense at that point—a gigantic obligation to a player at a time when the franchise was being put on the block. In fact, it was the Albert Belle signing that reinforced Peter's belief that baseball was, more than ever, a high-risk business. How does one player command $50-plus million when a team as valuable as the Dodgers may be worth only six times that amount?

There were, in my view, four major factors in Peter's decision to sell the Dodgers:

1. Escalating player salaries.

Exactly one week before Christmas, 1997, I received a memo from Graziano informing me "our 1998 budget requires us to hold player payroll at the same level as 1997, which was $49.3 million for the 40-man roster."

Player salaries and team payrolls around the majors were on the upswing, and I was being asked to watch the bottom line closer than ever before.

Our team payroll had been in the middle of the pack from 1994 through 1997, and yet we had responded with a combined record of 351-306, trailing only Atlanta, Cleveland, Baltimore and the New York Yankees in winning percentage over that period. And they all had much higher payrolls.

We were leading our division when the strike hit in 1994, reached postseason play in both 1995 and 1996, and carried our battle for the West Division title down to the final weekend in 1997.

Despite the payroll budget for 1998, we were anticipating being slightly in the black with a good season.

I always accepted the payroll I was given, even though I wasn't opposed to internal fights in the hopes of adding a key player or two at crucial points.

The tight financial policy wasn't limited to just the player payroll. A salary reduction plan was proposed for the management team as well. This ultimately was resolved with an incentive bonus plan (a potential of a six percent increase), leaving salary levels unchanged.

When the bonuses for management were first proposed, I was told I could receive a two percent pay increase if I kept the payroll under the stated limit. I refused the offer—my job was to fight for the best possible team.

2. The need for estate planning on the part of the O'Malley family.

"Peter and Terry (Seidler) combined have 13 children. A baseball team is not very liquid for those people," Graziano told *Time* magazine in January of 1997.

3. Peter's concern about the damage done to baseball by the 1994 strike and his own erosion of power in the sport's hierarchy.

Peter made his feelings very clear that the loss of the World Series was a major blow to baseball and that it would take years for the sport to recover.

Peter's own role in the decision-making process had been severely curtailed by Selig. Peter and the whole Dodger organization were being left out of the loop more and more. Dodger representation on the various committees was disappearing. Peter failed to gain a spot on the Executive Council even after having been nominated by National League president Bill White.

It was the small-market teams who were gaining power as Selig pushed forward with his consensus-building approach. Day by day, Peter seemed to be increasingly frustrated by the events taking place in baseball. The days when Bowie Kuhn was commissioner and Peter had a strong say were long gone.

4. The decision by Los Angeles mayor Richard Riordan to drop his support for a proposed NFL stadium next to Dodger Stadium.

When Mayor Riordan called Peter on August 22, 1995, asking the Dodger owner if he would help in bringing an NFL franchise back to Los Angeles, the event was so noteworthy that Peter saved the pink message slip. In fact, Peter is a great collector, and I would bet he still has the slip.

Peter and Bob Graziano turned a great deal of their attention to football. Unhappy with what was happening under Selig, Peter now had a new toy. And did he love that toy.

This was going to be Peter's way to leave a mark on the Los Angeles sports scene. Walter O'Malley had brought major league baseball to town. Now Peter was on a mission to bring the National Football League back to L.A.

After more than a year of devoting his time and energy to every detail of the NFL's return, and after having spent more than a million dollars in research and planning, Peter received word that Mayor Riordan had changed his mind. The mayor was throwing his support behind the Coliseum.

There is no question in my mind that the mayor's about-face on the NFL was, ultimately, the clinching factor of the four listed above in Peter's decision to sell.

If Peter had continued to receive the backing of the mayor and city officials to pursue his dream of an NFL franchise, it's very likely Los Angeles would have an NFL team today and the O'Malleys would still own the Dodgers.

"We basically sold (the Dodgers) because of football," O'Malley told Mark Whicker of the *Orange County Register* in August of 2002. "People think it's because the rest of the family wasn't interested in the Dodgers, but that was never an issue.

"We had a lot of exciting plans for the NFL here, and the elected officials (meaning ex-mayor Richard Riordan) talked us out of it. They were committed to the Coliseum, and in my mind, that was never a real alternative."

While Peter and his family may have had several reasons for selling the team, it is clear Rupert Murdoch had one driving motivation to buy the Dodgers—a regional sports television network in

Southern California. The race was on between Fox and Disney to establish such a network and, when the Dodgers were put up for sale, it was clear to Murdoch and his lieutenants that the historic baseball team could be the key and the foundation of their prized regional setup.

Disney officials had been thinking the same way for some time. Disney nearly had an agreement with the Dodgers to be part of a regional network in 1993. A five-year deal was in place for the Dodgers to join the Angels, Mighty Ducks and Clippers as part of such a network. All that was left was the signing of the final contract.

But at the last minute, Michael Eisner, chairman and CEO of Disney, asked the Dodgers for a five-year option. The Dodgers refused to go beyond the five-year term ending in 1998, and the deal was blown out of the water. Murdoch was determined to avoid such a disastrous breakdown.

Once Peter had announced the team was for sale, the only potential buyer receiving any attention was Fox. As the negotiations were just warming up, there was a story in *Newsday* in mid-May that I would be dismissed after the sale was completed. Fox officials responded to that story by issuing a press release, even though they had not yet gained ownership of the team.

"Fred Claire—as well as other members of the Dodger family—have built one of the most successful and respected organizations in the history of professional sports," said the release. "Claire's record speaks for itself—including his role in developing each of the last five National League Rookies of the Year—a Major League record.

"Pending a successful sales process, the FOX Group would certainly welcome Claire's vast experience and class to the FOX family, as well as that of the rest of the Dodgers' front office. We find today's (May 19) *Newsday* article false and in extremely poor taste."

Things were certainly getting interesting in the new corporate environment of the Dodgers, even before the "For Sale" sign had been taken down.

As matters developed, it was clear baseball's owners weren't going to turn down the opportunity to welcome Fox as a new partner. The sale, for $311 million, was approved on March 19, 1998 at an owners' meeting in St. Petersburg, Fla.

Several Fox officials—including Chase Carey and Peter Chernin—flew to Dodgertown to hold a press conference. "We want to continue the great Los Angeles Dodger tradition," Carey said. "Our goal is to have a smooth transition."

I showed Carey and Chernin around the complex, including the Dodger locker room, where all of the uniforms were neatly hung in place for the next day's activity.

Little did I know that, a few months later, Carey himself would make a trade that would remove Mike Piazza's No. 31 from that clubhouse.

CHAPTER XIX

FOX IS IN,
PIAZZA IS OUT

From the front office to the dugout to the cheap seats, all concerned watched the calm seas under new Dodger management and wondered what waves of change would eventually wash over them.

They had less than two months to wait. On May 15, the new owners unleashed a tsunami from which the Dodgers have yet to recover, the course and structure of the team forever altered.

On that date, catcher Mike Piazza, one of the most popular and explosive players to ever wear Dodger Blue, was traded to the Florida Marlins as part of a seven-player deal.

There have been shocking trades before, but never one orchestrated by a television executive whose first priority was to improve a team's lineup of stations rather than its batting lineup.

The deal, which sent Piazza and third baseman Todd Zeile to the Marlins for outfielders Gary Sheffield and Jim Eisenreich, infielder Bobby Bonilla, catcher Charles Johnson and minor-league pitcher Manuel Barrios, was struck without even the courtesy of informing me, the Dodger general manager.

Instead, incredibly, it was orchestrated by Fox television executive Chase Carey as part of his pursuit of a regional sports channel in Florida. Carey wanted the Marlins to be part of that venture. It's true. This seven-player trade was, first and foremost, a television deal.

Television rights had always been important to the O'Malley-owned Dodgers. No one was more of a visionary than Walter O'Malley when it came to baseball and TV. But the O'Malley Dodgers never would have let television rights impact a baseball decision.

My reaction to the trade cost me my position with the Dodgers. The trade cost the Dodgers much more: Their franchise player, and, more importantly over the long run, their credibility.

After all, prior to the approval of the sale, Fox executives had assured baseball owners there would be a "wall" between their television business and the baseball business. In one trade, that wall came tumbling down.

How did that happen?

The first thing one needs to understand about Fox's purchase of the Dodgers is that it was an investment triggered by the company's desire to establish a regional sports network in Southern California. Fox, however, had competition for such a network in the Disney Corporation. It was the purchase of the Dodgers that ultimately enabled Fox to edge out Disney.

The stunning part of all this is how Piazza got caught up in the wires of this television deal. It wasn't logical. Not with Fox involved. After all, if there is one thing Fox executives understand, it's entertainment. And Mike has true star quality in the baseball universe.

But the new team owner simply did not understand the structure of a baseball team and the importance of a franchise player.

In fairness to the folks at Fox, they found themselves in an awkward position when they purchased the team because Mike was eligible to become a free agent at the close of that 1998 season.

The last thing Fox wanted was a bidding war over Mike, and the embarrassing possibility that the team's most popular player would choose to depart. That certainly wouldn't have been a very good start for Fox. Incredibly, they managed to make it an even worse start.

The fact is, Fox was worried about the Piazza contract situation even before the company officially took over the baseball team.

Back in October of 1997, Dan Lozano, Mike's agent, had established a mid-February deadline for signing the superstar catcher. Imagine our surprise when that plan was outlined in a story in the *L.A. Times* before we had heard this bit of news from Lozano himself.

I was having breakfast at the L.A. Police Academy one morning when I read the following Lozano quote in the *Times*: "I want to stress this isn't a threat, but our approach is going to be that something absolutely has to be done before February 15. We would like Mike to go into next season with a clear mind so that he can concentrate on having another great year. If we don't get something done by February 15, Mike will play out the year and test the free-agent market."

I thought to myself, is this amazing or what? This is the type of thing where you could put the agent and player in a terrible P.R. position by their actions—telling the press before telling the club.

I resolved the situation with Lozano in a telephone call, telling him it was important we handle these negotiations in such a way as to not damage Mike. There are times when you need to do everything you can to protect the image and the position of the player while still having the team's objective in mind.

On February 4, 1998, a meeting on Mike's status was held at the Fox offices in Los Angeles. Attending on behalf of the Dodgers were executive vice-president Bob Graziano, attorney Sam Fernandez and I. Representing Murdoch were Fox News Corp. executives Peter Chernin and Carey.

Midway through the meeting, we were joined by Murdoch himself. Chernin and Carey brought him up to date on the Piazza contract, explaining that Mike was signed through 1998, but was eligible for free agency at the end of the season and would probably become baseball's highest-paid player.

Murdoch suggested that perhaps we could get Mike to sign an option for future seasons. Sam explained this wasn't workable in a baseball contract.

"These guys are worse than movie stars," Murdoch responded, and then left to take care of what I presumed to be more pressing business.

The contract situation related to Mike was rather basic. The highest-paid player in the game entering 1998 was Boston pitcher Pedro Martinez. In December of 1997, Martinez had signed a six-year deal worth $75 million. The contract averaged $12.5 million per season, plus a $5 million bonus tied to Martinez winning the Cy Young Award. There also was an option for the 2004 season for $17.5 million, with a $2.5 million buyout.

Following Martinez in the salary standings was Greg Maddux (an average of $11.5 million per season), followed by Barry Bonds ($11.450), Albert Belle ($11), Sammy Sosa ($10.625) and Gary Sheffield ($10.167).

The Martinez figure of $12.5 million was the benchmark. We realized we were going to have to top that figure in order to have a chance to sign Piazza.

We received the blessing of Chernin and Carey to proceed with the negotiations, Sam being designated as our point man in dealing with Lozano.

Sam arranged a meeting and came armed with a contract: $12.6 million a year for six years. Lozano had wanted something in writing and he had it, a contract that would make Mike the highest-paid player in the game on the basis of average annual salary.

Lozano listened to Sam's offer, examined the contract and finally responded, with regret in his voice, "Mike is going to be disappointed."

Lozano's goal was to make Mike the first $100 million-player and he was willing to go to seven years to break that barrier. Lozano realized his mid-February deadline wasn't practical since Fox didn't even figure to be in control of the team by then.

February turned into March, spring training was in full bloom in Vero Beach, but the lid remained firmly on negotiations. Mike gave all the right answers to the media, leaving them with a non-story on the contract front.

A few days after the announcement that Fox officially owned the Dodgers, Sam received a counteroffer from Lozano: eight years at $18 million a season, a hotel suite on the road, and a luxury box between the bases with Mike having the option to purchase that box at a later date.

It was the type of offer you just write down because there is no verbal response that makes sense. A few days later, Sam responded, making it clear to Lozano we did want to sign Mike, but there was a lot of work to be done to even get to the area of a reasonable deal.

With the regular season about to start, Sam and Lozano agreed that "no comment" was the best reply to any media questions about their negotiations.

The groundwork seemed to be in place to strike a deal. But then the negotiations unraveled just as we were unwrapping the start of the regular season.

After we lost our opening day game in St. Louis, Mike told Jason Reid of the *Los Angeles Times*, "I'm not going to lie and say I'm not concerned about this, that I'm not confused and disappointed by the whole thing, because I am. I'm mad that this has dragged into the season and that it now has the potential to become a distraction...How can I not think about this?"

It was a terrible mistake by Mike, in my view, to publicly air his complaints. Here we were starting our season, Mike was earning $8 million as part of a two-year, $15-million deal and he already had received an offer that would boost him up to the top of the big-league money list. When the story of our season opener turned out to be Mike's unhappiness, the president of the Dodgers felt a response was necessary.

This was a new Dodger president because Graziano had replaced Peter O'Malley with the sale of the team. Peter had agreed to accept a position as chairman of the board, but, for the first time in 30 years, he wasn't at the controls.

With the opener followed by a day off, our team had a workout at Busch Stadium. I spent much of the morning at the stadium on a conference call with Graziano and Fernandez.

Bob wanted to draft a strong response to Mike's comments and it was determined Sam would be the spokesman in the Dodger press release. That was fine with me since I wasn't comfortable with the wording being used. It was clear the response was not going to be in keeping with the way Peter O'Malley and I had normally done business.

When I arrived at Busch Stadium for an afternoon game the next day and entered our clubhouse, it didn't take long to see Mike was an unhappy camper. Headed to the field with a couple of bats in his hands, the look on Mike's face would have put fear in the heart of any opposing pitcher.

But this was more than a game face. This was an angry face. I wasn't in the best of moods myself in that I felt Mike's statements after opening day had created a distraction that wasn't necessary.

I told Derrick Hall, our publicity director, to let Mike know I wanted to meet with him in an isolated room near the clubhouse as soon as he was finished with his pregame routine.

As Mike entered that room, he wasted no time on pleasantries. He was upset about the Dodgers' statement, which had appeared in the L.A. papers that morning, and he wanted me to know it.

The statement, quoting Sam, reiterated the Dodgers' desire to sign Mike, then added, "Unfortunately, to date, we have not been able to bridge the wide gap that exists between our respective positions, primarily because, at this point in the negotiations, there is no good way for either side to accurately assess the level of compensation that a player of Mike's caliber can command in today's market."

"I want to get this contract settled or I want out of here," Mike told me in no uncertain terms. "You guys are low-balling me. I admit we're high with our offer, but I want to get this thing settled."

Now, it was my turn.

"First of all, Mike, we are not low-balling you," I said. "When you are offered the type of contract we offered you, don't put a low-ball tag on that. Furthermore, your statements on opening day were not good for you and not good for this team.

"I'm disappointed in you. We're just starting out this season. We don't need that bullshit."

"I want to know what you guys want to do," Mike snapped back. "Either sign me or get me out of here."

I told Mike I would meet with Graziano and we would get back to him and Lozano and let them know exactly where we stood. Mike cooled off and went on his way.

After the two games in St. Louis, we headed to Cincinnati for a weekend series and then returned home.

The first order of business on Monday morning, April 6, was a meeting at the Fox studios to discuss the Piazza situation. It was an interesting drive from Dodger Stadium to Fox. Here was Peter O'Malley, the former owner, leaving Dodger Stadium to drive to the headquarters of the new owner. Peter drove his Mercedes and I was seated with him in the front seat, with Graziano and Fernandez in the back.

"This is my first meeting as the Dodger chairman of the board," said Peter in a very relaxed manner.

At Fox, we headed to a conference room to meet with Chernin and Carey. Sam and I provided the background on our discussions with Lozano and Piazza.

When Chernin asked for recommendations on how to proceed, I said we definitely should do everything we could to sign Mike. I made a strong push, even though I realized our payroll already stood at $48.5 million, the limit I had been given, and I was advocating a contract that would push that figure much higher over the following few seasons.

Later in the day, we made what turned out to be our final offer to Mike: $13.5 million for six years, a total package of $81 million. We said we were open to increasing the offer by way of an option for a seventh year. Lozano later responded with what was to be the final offer on behalf of Mike: $15 million for seven years, a total of $105 million.

We clearly had a gap, but at that point, there still seemed to be plenty of time to close it. There was a season to be played, and there would be a period after the season in which we would have the exclusive rights to negotiate with Mike.

By midweek, we discussed a joint statement to put the contract story to rest, but ended up with two statements.

"I have instructed my agent, Dan Lozano, to shut down contract negotiations with the Dodgers," said Mike in his statement. "I let the talks become a distraction, and for that, I apologize to my teammates and our fans. For the rest of this season, I will focus completely on bringing a championship to Los Angeles and will not discuss my contract status with anyone until the season ends."

I issued a statement on behalf of the Dodgers, declaring, "We concur with Mike Piazza's decision, and we look forward to negotiating with Mike and his agent at the conclusion of the season."

It looked as though the Piazza contract situation had been successfully packed up and put away with a label that read, "Do not open until October."

The shelf life of that label, however, turned out to be less than one week.

Several days after I thought I could shift my full attention to the new season, I received a telephone call from Florida Marlin general manager Dave Dombrowski. That call ultimately led to the departure of Mike Piazza. Both Piazza and Lozano were stunned. Neither man saw it coming.

Neither did I—the team's general manager.

Postscript: On October 26, 1998, the New York Mets signed Mike Piazza to a record seven-year contract for $91 million. At an average of $13 million a season, Piazza's contract was the richest in baseball, surpassing Martinez's $12.5 million salary.

Even so, Mike's deal fell short of the $13.5 million average annual salary we had offered in our final proposal.

CHAPTER XX

THE PIAZZA TRADE...
OUT OF THE BLUE

In my years as Dodger general manager, I used a scorebook during games. The routine came from my days as a writer, and I also found it useful in my role as GM. My scorebook would usually be marked with an assortment of notes that would prove invaluable when I later reviewed the game.

When I look back on my scorebook of 1998, a home game against Philadelphia at Dodger Stadium on May 14 comes to an abrupt end in the bottom of the eighth inning. As it turned out, that also marked the beginning of the end of my career with the Dodgers. My last entry shows Jose Vizcaino coming to bat with Todd Hollandsworth on first base and the Dodgers trailing 2-0.

It was at that point that I received a call from team president Bob Graziano. Bob was calling from the Dominican Republic, but I could hear him very clearly. I just found it hard to believe what he was saying.

"Fred, we have made a trade that needs to be announced tonight," he told me. "We have acquired Gary Sheffield, Charles Johnson, Bobby Bonilla and Jim Eisenreich for Mike Piazza and Todd Zeile."

Talk about stunning news. Here I was, general manager of the Dodgers, being informed of a trade already consummated that was to change both our franchise and our financial structure in a dramatic way. I could barely believe what I was hearing, but I did have an immediate response.

"Bob," I said, "there will be two announcements tonight, because I will have an announcement to make on my status after the trade is announced. With this trade, you don't need me."

"I wish I could be there to deal with this directly, but I was caught by surprise," Graziano admitted.

Graziano later told me Fox wanted me to say I had made the trade. But, when Bob heard my response upon being informed of the done deal, he knew there was no use making that request of me.

Graziano said he believed the Marlin players were aware of the deal, but he had concerns about telling our players at that point.

"Bob, I'm going downstairs to tell our two players as soon as this game ends," I said forcefully. "If you think I'm going to have them hear this news on the radio, you're wrong."

Piazza had been with our organization for a decade and Zeile had signed with us for less than market value because he wanted to play for the Dodgers and be near his Southern California home.

I asked Derrick Hall, our publicity director, to come to my box and handed him the phone so he could coordinate the details of the announcement with Graziano.

I returned to my office, leaving my box before the end of a game for the first time I could recall. My world had just been turned upside down. I was learning of a Dodger trade instead of putting the deal together.

I'll never forget sitting in that office, looking around the room and thinking of so many memories and realizing nothing would ever be the same again for me with the Dodgers.

Before too much time had passed, my phone rang. It was Derrick, telling me there could be no announcement that night because Sheffield had a no-trade clause in his contract. When Bob had informed me of the trade, I assumed the no-trade provision had been dealt with by whoever was now at the controls.

I went down to the Dodger clubhouse just as the game ended and into the office of Dr. Frank Jobe, an office just off our training room that afforded some privacy. I told Charlie Strasser, our trainer, to make sure Piazza and Zeile didn't leave the clubhouse until I had a chance to talk to them.

Mike and Todd had showered and dressed when they came into Dr. Jobe's office. I had Derrick with me. I told the two players they had been traded to the Marlins, but the trade wasn't complete until one of the Marlin players agreed to waive his no-trade clause.

Mike immediately saw beyond the shocking news I had hit him with.

"Who are we going to?" he said. "The Marlins aren't going to keep us."

"I don't know, Mike," I replied. "That will be up to the Marlins."

Mike had another question: "Who have we been traded for?"

"I can't tell you," I responded. "It wouldn't be fair if the Marlin players haven't heard the news and I don't want to be responsible for letting out the word when a player may not know. That's the very thing I'm trying to protect here."

"You can't tell me or you don't know?" Mike persisted.

"I can't tell you," I said.

As Mike and Todd walked out of the office, Mike said something about "a slice of heaven." Todd didn't say a word. He understood what had happened and he was stunned. I couldn't blame him one bit.

Upon arriving in Florida, Mike and Todd would live together in a home owned by Mike.

"I'm going to go into his bedroom and scream at him every morning at 4 a.m.," Zeile told friends. "The only reason I ended up in Florida is because he didn't sign."

I awoke the next morning to news blasting from every radio station in Los Angeles—Mike Piazza had been traded. Only the details remained to be worked out, the media reported.

As I drove from my Pasadena home to Dodger Stadium, Gary Sheffield and his agent, Jim Neader, were en route to Los Angeles. Sheffield was flying in from St. Louis, where the Marlins were playing the Cardinals.

When I reached my office, I learned the plan was for Sheffield to be met at LAX by a limo, driven to the Fox Studios to say hello to Fox officials, and then to be delivered to Dodger Stadium where we were to work out what Fox officials seemed to think were nagging little details holding the trade up.

They were hardly little. In fact, there was no deal until Sheffield gave his approval. The no-trade clause in his contract gave him complete control of the situation. Despite my initial reaction to Graziano, I realized this was not the time to bid goodbye to the Dodgers. We had a mess to clean up.

It made no sense to try to turn back the clock. The no-trade issue needed to be resolved and the deal needed to be completed. There was no way to put all of this back into a neat package.

On the other side of the country, Dombrowski was discovering his package wasn't quite signed and sealed either. He called me that morning to inform me he had learned one of five young Marlin pitchers was to be included in the trade.

And, further stunning me, he told me the pitcher was to be selected by the Marlins.

Why would they be giving us five names if they had the right to select the player? Why not simply name that player?

Dave told me he had not been aware of this aspect of the deal, and that he didn't really want to part with any of these five pitchers. He asked if I would consider another player. I told him I also knew nothing about this part of the deal, but that we would look at the five. Dave, realizing he was going to have to part with one of them, called me back to say that righthander Manuel Barrios would be the one we'd receive.

I went to lunch with Sam Fernandez, and we discussed the bizarre events that had unfolded. I had called Sam the previous night at his home to tell him of Graziano's call. Sam couldn't believe what had transpired.

When Sam and I returned from lunch, I had a surprise visitor waiting for me. It was Chase Carey, the Fox executive who had pulled the trigger on the deal. Chase told me he thought I had been more in the loop about the negotiations. I told Carey the only knowledge I had came from a call I had received from Marlin general manager Dave Dombrowski shortly after the season opened.

In that call, on April 10, our negotiations with Piazza on hold, Dombrowski had inquired about Mike. His approach was very direct—"Fred, would you trade Mike Piazza and a young, low-salaried pitcher for Charles Johnson, Gary Sheffield and Jim Eisenreich?"

I knew Dombrowski was under orders from Florida owner Wayne Huizenga to unload payroll after the Marlins had won the World Series the previous season and yet had lost money in the process. Sheffield was at the top of the Marlin salary list in that he had just signed a six-year deal that paid him $61 million from 1998 through 2003.

Dombrowski figured if he could trade Sheffield for Piazza, the Marlins would be free of the bulk of their future payroll obligations. Furthermore, Dombrowski would be in a position to acquire young players for Piazza in that Mike was in the last year of his contract.

I went to Graziano and told him of Dombrowski's call. I told Bob I wanted to reply to Dombrowski that we weren't interested in discussing Piazza because we wanted to sign Mike, but we were interested in Sheffield.

My reasoning: I felt that, as long as Sheffield remained the focus of trade discussions, Johnson would remain a Marlin. The two made an attractive package, the high-priced slugger teamed with a lower-priced but highly valuable catcher. If Fox ultimately decided Piazza had to go, Johnson would be just the replacement we needed.

I also knew that, if I returned Dombrowski's call and told him we were interested in trading Mike, this bit of information would be major news before the day was over. Talk about a potential season-shattering distraction. It's nearly impossible to keep this type of trade discussion under wraps.

Besides, there was a rumor in the press that Piazza's father, Vince, had an interest in buying the Marlins. If you had the chance to move $61 million of payroll obligation, this figured to reach the ears of a potential buyer. And if that potential buyer's son was the central figure in the payroll shift…well, no telling where all that would lead or how it would affect our club.

I called Dombrowski back, with Graziano's approval, and told him we would have an interest in Sheffield if the Marlins would resolve the "no trade" clause in his contract and also pay $3 million a year of his contract. Dave responded by saying the Marlins would take back part of the contract, but he doubted it would be to the tune of $3 million a year.

That was as far as I went in any discussion of a trade for Gary Sheffield. And at no time did I discuss the possibility of trading Piazza to the Marlins or to any other team. Now, here was Chase Carey sitting in my office saying he felt I was far more tuned in to the trade than I actually had been.

I hadn't known Chase very long, but I liked him. Still, that didn't stop me from telling him that, if he was going to start making deals, he should become the general manager. If that didn't interest him, I said, he should let me do my job. He seemed to respect my feelings.

Dombrowski later assured me he hadn't gone over my head to have discussions with anyone from Fox. I told Dave that thought had never entered my mind and that I respected him as a general manager.

But I was clearly upset about what had transpired on my end of the deal, and I made no effort to camouflage my feelings. I didn't feel this was the way to run a baseball team. I didn't feel the trade had been handled properly. I expressed those feelings to several sportswriters. I was quoted in the *New York Times* comparing working for Fox with working for Yankee owner George Steinbrenner. I didn't mean it as a flattering comparison.

Bob Keisser, a Long Beach columnist, warned me that Fox officials were upset with my remarks, but that didn't dissuade me.

The amazing part of the trade is that Graziano and I were to have met with Fox executive Peter Chernin two nights later to discuss Piazza's status. I was developing a strategy and a list of teams that I felt might be interested in Piazza if Fox gave the order to trade Mike. The key point in my mind is that there was no urgency to make such a move. We had a couple of months before the trading deadline of July 31 to evaluate our chances for postseason play and to quietly explore the market for Mike without triggering wild rumors.

In spite of all of my careful handling, here was the deal exploding in my face. Furthermore, we had taken on the salary of Bobby Bonilla, who was making $5.9 million a year for three seasons.

Even Eisenreich was making $1.4 million in 1998 with an option for the same figure in 1999. Add in Sheffield, and it meant we had taken on an obligation of $80.1 million for three players. The Dodgers' total payroll for 1998 was $48.5 million, and I had been instructed by Graziano not to go one dollar over that amount.

Sheffield and Neader entered my office on the night of May 15 just as our game was about to begin. I couldn't help but think about how strange it all was.

Here was one of the Marlins' key players, sitting in my office at Dodger Stadium while his team was playing a game in St. Louis. Furthermore, neither Piazza nor Zeile had reported to Dodger Stadium that night due to the reports of the trade, despite my pleas to their agents to have the players in attendance.

The first words Sheffield spoke actually put me in step with him. "I want to either get this done or get back to the Marlins," he said. "This isn't fair to the other players involved, my teammates, and Mike and Todd."

It took a baseball player to realize what this was all about. I told Gary I agreed with his assessment and that we wanted to get the deal completed. I acknowledged that he held the key in that he had the no-trade clause. I assured Gary that, by the time our meeting ended, he would either be a Dodger or would be headed back to the Marlins that night.

Neader spoke up, saying that, if Gary approved the trade, he would face additional personal expenses due to the difference in state income tax laws between Florida and California. The agent added there would also be additional expenses related to Gary establishing a residence in L.A. and having his family travel to and from Florida.

Graziano and Fernandez had joined me in my office for the meeting. We all knew we had our hands full. We were going to have to pay to complete the deal and the only question was how much.

We reached Carey and Chernin, on their way to a social function with Murdoch, to update them. We also placed a call to a very unhappy Don Smiley, the Marlins' president, who said he had told Carey about the no-trade clause when the two had made the deal. Smiley's position was, that made the no-trade stipulation the Dodgers' problem.

Ultimately we reached a settlement. Sheffield would be paid $5.5 million to waive his no-trade clause. The Marlins would pick up $2.5 million of that amount.

The other game taking place—the one on the field below my office—was just about to end. I called Derrick Hall and told him to arrange a press conference in the Stadium Club.

As we left my office to head for the Stadium Club, I told Gary I didn't want him to be surprised by what I planned to say at the press conference. I wanted him to know that, regardless of my remarks, I would give him my full support and was confident he could help the Dodgers.

In the Stadium Club, Derrick formally announced the deal. When I took the microphone, I told the media throng before me, "I want to be perfectly clear on how I learned of this trade. I received a telephone call from Bob Graziano in the Dominican Republic."

I wasn't about to stand before the news media and, in essence, the fans, and talk about the details of a trade I didn't engineer. My response to the trade ultimately cost me my job with the Dodgers, according to those who were close to the folks at Fox.

For what it's worth, I would respond the same way today.

Postscript: Here is Dombrowski's account of the trade — *"The Marlin ownership kept me in informed of the possibility of a Piazza trade. I was involved step by step. They kept coming back, asking me what they should do. It didn't bother me that I was not the spokesman. You have to remember what we were trying to accomplish, that was to cut payroll. I knew Piazza would be easy to move.*

"I felt bad from Fred's perspective, but we all end up in situations beyond our control, and my concern was the Florida Marlins. In today's game, when you are talking about such large dollars, ownership gets involved to some extent. But the circumstances of that trade, with Fred not being included at all, were one of the most unusual I've seen in my career."

CHAPTER XXI

MY FINAL TRADE

The Piazza trade was done. Now, it was my turn to deal. I didn't plan on being gun shy because of the manner in which the trade had been consummated. Just the opposite. I planned on taking aim at another big target: the Seattle Mariners' Randy Johnson, considered by many to be baseball's premier lefthander.

I had two good reasons for zeroing in on Johnson: 1) We had just made a blockbuster deal that clearly showed Fox's desire to win at all costs in 1998, and 2) I had been talking with righthander Hideo Nomo and his agent, Don Nomura, about Nomo's unhappiness over remaining in a Dodger uniform.

So on May 26, just 11 days after the completion of the Piazza deal, I made my first call to Seattle general manager Woody Woodward to inquire about Johnson.

I figured, if the Mariners would trade Johnson for Nomo and one of our younger players—perhaps second baseman Wilton Guerrero, who had previously been sought by Seattle—I could close the deal that would get us into the postseason.

To me, the trade made all the sense in the world. Unhappy Hideo was making $2.8 million a year. Guerrero was making $200,000 and was expendable. Johnson, making $6 million, would be a free agent at season's end.

The cost to the Dodgers, with a third of the season already gone, would be around $2 million.

On the road in Houston, I called Graziano at Dodger Stadium to get clearance to proceed since I would be adding $2 million to the payroll. I figured that was a small bump compared to the $10 million Fox had already added as a result of the Piazza trade.

"Fred," Graziano told me, "you can proceed with the trade discussion, but there are two key points. Fox wants Johnson to have a physical, and I realize that's a little strange in that the Marlin players weren't asked to take physicals (especially since Bonilla was coming off surgery on both his wrist and Achilles tendon).

"And, Fox is worried about Guerrero being traded in that he is regarded as the next Dodger second baseman."

Another news bulletin to me from Fox.

"Fox may see Wilton as our next second baseman, Bob," I said, "but we have an outstanding player signed in Eric Young, and the majority of our baseball people would place Adam Riggs ahead of Wilton at second base."

I could tell Graziano was a little uneasy, but he told me to pursue the deal.

The Mariners were in Florida that day to play the Marlins. I placed two calls to Woodward's hotel room during our game against Houston, but there was no answer. I left a message, telling him it was important that I talk to him by the following morning.

I knew Woodward wasn't going to make a deal for Johnson before he heard what I had to say.

Returning home from Houston with the team that night, Sheryl and I didn't get to bed until 2 a.m.

One hour later, the phone rang.

It was Nomura calling from Japan. An internet service was carrying a story by baseball writer Bob Nightengale that Nomo and Todd Hollandsworth had been traded to Seattle for Randy Johnson.

"Is the deal done?" Nomura asked. "Should I fly to Los Angeles?"

Not an easy question to answer at 3 a.m. or any other time under the circumstances.

"Don," I told him, "there has been no trade. I haven't mentioned Hideo's name to Seattle or to any other team (true at that point), but we do have an interest in Randy Johnson. You'll have to decide if you want to fly to Los Angeles."

As I hung up, I wondered how the information had leaked. The only person with whom I had shared my idea of Nomo for Johnson was Graziano. It was unusual for me not to discuss such a deal with our manager, coaches and scouts, but I didn't want word to leak out and I felt confident everybody in our organization would be strongly in favor of such a trade.

Graziano later told me the only person he had passed the trade possibility on to was Chase Carey.

Where did Nightengale get his information?

The following morning, Woodward and I finally made contact. I told him we wanted to proceed with discussions about Johnson, but didn't mention any players I'd be willing to give up.

Woody gave me a proposal: Third baseman Adrian Beltre and pitcher Darren Dreifort for Johnson.

If we weren't interested, Woody said, there were other clubs he felt obligated to talk to about Johnson. I told him I thought it was best he got started on those calls because Beltre and Dreifort weren't going anywhere.

When batting practice began late that afternoon at Dodger Stadium prior to our game against Cincinnati, the field was full of media people. Topic No. 1: Randy Johnson.

As I watched the scene before me, I imagined how much bigger the media mob would have been if the subject of the rumors had been the Mike Piazza trade before it became reality.

The Johnson rumors remained on everybody's lips throughout the weekend, but another element entered the equation on Saturday evening when I got another call from Nomura. He wanted to know if he and Nomo could meet with Peter O'Malley and me the following morning at 10 a.m. Just hours earlier, Nomo had had a rather uninspired outing in losing to Cincinnati.

When we met in Peter's office, Nomura was blunt. He was requesting a trade on behalf of Nomo. The pitcher, said Nomura, simply wasn't happy pitching for the Dodgers, didn't feel the team had confidence in him and wanted to go to a "team that had a chance to win."

This wasn't the first time I had heard this. Nomura and Nomo had held a meeting with me at our team hotel in Chicago back in April to express the same sentiments.

This time, a plan was agreed upon. A press conference would be held the following day to enable Nomo to publicly state his desire to be traded. We didn't need any more rumors, we didn't need the press hounding Nomo. It was better to be up front about this.

The following morning, I held a conference call with Russell and our coaches to alert everyone about what was going on. The news didn't go over well because it was felt that we, as an organization, had reached out and done everything possible to please and help Nomo.

"You know what we should do?" said coach Reggie Smith. "We should send his butt to Albuquerque."

When I heard that suggestion, I thought, "Bingo."

Here we have a player who doesn't want to be a Dodger, and his unhappiness has stretched over at least six weeks with little improvement in his performance.

I met with Graziano and told him I had decided on a course of action, a rather unusual course of action. I planned to designate Nomo's contract for assignment, meaning we had 10 days to trade him, outright the contract (whereby he could have declared free agency if not claimed by another team), or simply release him (I was certain it wouldn't come to that).

Graziano said to go ahead. Peter was informed. I don't believe Graziano told anyone at Fox. According to an article in *ESPN The Magazine*, Peter Chernin had learned of the move from writer Diane K. Shah.

When Nomo and Nomura arrived at my office, expecting to be led to the press conference, I told them there had been a change of plans: Nomo had been designated for assignment. He was no longer on the Dodger roster. The press conference was held as scheduled. But the announcement was the last thing Nomo had expected to hear.

Mission accomplished. You don't want to play for the Dodgers? You are no longer a Dodger. Nomura later wrote me to say he thought it was "a bold and yet brilliant move," one of the nicer compliments I ever received from an agent. Some members of the media were not so kind, saying I had diminished Nomo's value. A Fox official called Ross Newhan of the *L.A. Times* to question the deal. Nothing like a little support from the home office.

I also heard from my fellow general managers. By the time I returned to my office, eight of them had called to express interest in Nomo.

I felt like an agent as I took calls from the GMs. I told them I was looking for pitching, either a starter, setup man or closer.

There were some very interesting possibilities. Baltimore and Cleveland both called, a welcome development, since both had outstanding relief. Kansas City called to mention my old buddy, Tim Belcher, but then called back to say two of their scouts had doubts about Nomo. Texas was offering Bobby Witt, who would subsequently be released by the Rangers shortly thereafter. Toronto mentioned Erik Hanson, who would also wind up being released.

The one club willing to talk about a number of their pitchers was the New York Mets.

I felt we had a fit there for several reasons. The Mets had already developed a tie with Japan, having signed pitcher Masato Yoshii, a former teammate and good friend of Nomo. Mets manager Bobby Valentine had managed in Japan. And Dave Wallace, an assistant to Met general manager Steve Phillips, had been Nomo's pitching coach with the Dodgers.

One of our scouts, John Barr, also a former Met scout, told me he felt the Mets would make every effort to obtain Nomo.

So I felt I could depend on them and soon realized I was going to need them as the market for Nomo moved south. The 10-day clock on designation was ticking and nothing was happening with all of the other supposedly interested clubs.

It was time to call Phillips.

I did so on June 4, offering to trade Nomo for pitcher Dave Mlicki, who had been in and out of the rotation, and reliever Greg McMichael, a name the Mets hadn't previously mentioned as trade bait.

Our scouts liked both Mlicki and McMichael and realized this was the best deal possible.

Craig Wright, whom I used during my tenure as GM for his excellent statistical analysis of players, made the point that Mlicki always pitched better when he was in the regular rotation, starting every five days. His ERA was a full run better during those periods.

Our scouts felt Mlicki was better served using his sinking fastball more and not throwing as many breaking pitches. We knew he had a good arm, but he wasn't using his fastball enough.

McMichael had a great palm ball and the frame of mind to pitch late in games. He wasn't a high-velocity guy, but I knew he was trying to establish his fastball more on the inside part of the plate to make his palm ball more effective.

It was to be my last trade as Dodger general manager, and one that was symbolic of the way I tried to approach every trade—listen to your manager, coaching staff and, most importantly, your scouts. Then, pull the trigger and take responsibility.

CHAPTER XXII

SEE ME—POM

On the night I was fired, I thought it probably would be awhile before I had any further conversations with Peter O'Malley.

It turned out to be less than 12 hours.

On Monday, June 22, the morning after I had been let go, I received a call from Peter at my home. He told me he had a press conference to attend that afternoon and wanted to know if I was available for lunch.

"Sometimes," he told me, "you need to bounce things off of people in situations like this."

The only thing I felt I needed to do was bounce back and start making the best of the rest of my life. The reality of the previous night hit me when I went out into the driveway, picked up my *L.A. Times* and found my picture on the front page under the heading, "Dodgers Fire Claire, Russell."

I told Peter I already had a busy day planned. My daughters, Jennifer and Kimberly, were taking me to a belated Father's Day lunch since I had been in Denver the day before.

So a luncheon before the press conference was out, but Peter said he still wanted to meet with me. With his schedule tight because of an upcoming trip to Ireland, he suggested the following day.

I told him I thought it would be better if we waited awhile.

And then I added, "Besides, Peter, you don't get involved with firing people who have worked for you for 30 years. It's not good business."

Nevertheless, at the news conference where the appointments of Glenn Hoffman as manager and Tommy Lasorda as GM were announced, Peter volunteered the information that, if he were still in control of the club, Bill Russell and I would have suffered the same fate. I feel Peter made that statement to show support for the Fox regime, but I think nearly everyone at that news conference knew Peter wouldn't have handled our dismissals in that fashion.

In fact, I was later told that a longtime department head called Peter the day after the press conference and left a simple, but direct message: "Peter, I don't believe you."

Off Peter went to Ireland. When he returned, he again called and we agreed on lunch for July 22, a month and a day after my firing. We would meet at the Parkway Grill in Pasadena, an easy drive from both my home and Dodger Stadium.

And so we met, two men who had worked together for 30 years and had always enjoyed a candid relationship. It was a relationship I thought about as I drove to lunch. There were so many great memories involving the Dodgers and Peter.

It was Peter who prodded Red Patterson into selecting me to be publicity director when I first joined the Dodgers in 1969.

It was Peter, with the approval of his father, Walter, who appointed me VP of public relations and promotions when Red left after the 1974 season to become president of the Angels.

It was Peter who promoted me to executive vice-president in 1982, a title that hadn't been used since Peter himself held that position under his father.

Fred is flanked by Walt Alston and Peter O'Malley (with a young Bobby Valentine in front) at Baseball Writers Dinner in 1975.

And it was Peter who asked me to take over the responsibility for baseball operations after Al Campanis was forced to resign in 1987.

Life was much simpler in my early days with the team for both owners and executives. Those were the days before free agency and soaring salaries. The marketing of the game was making great strides, and Peter turned to me to direct the Dodger effort in that area.

During that period, it wasn't unusual for Peter to take a group of team executives to Wilshire Country Club for a round of golf when the team left on a road trip. Quite often, the foursome consisted of Peter, ticket manager Walter Nash, stadium operations director Bob Smith and me. Between the four of us, we knew almost everything that was transpiring on the business side of the club and could resolve any questions over the 18 holes.

There was very little that escaped Peter's attention. When something crossed his desk that raised a thought or question, he would scribble "See Me—POM" on the paper and pass it along to the proper department head. I was the league leader in what became known as "See Mes." I got so many, I kept a folder on my desk titled, "See Me—POM."

There were very few working days in my first two decades with the team that I didn't meet with Peter. I felt honored he trusted me with so much responsibility. His support of me was unwavering.

Early in 1977, while at lunch with Nash and Smith at Nikola's Restaurant on Sunset Boulevard near Dodger Stadium, I made the bold prediction that we would become the first major league team to draw three million fans and that we would do it that season. Nash and Smith disagreed.

A wager was made and it wasn't long before word of the bet spread around the Dodger offices. The word, as always, didn't bypass Peter's office.

One day shortly after, I found a box on my desk with a note attached by scotch tape. The note read, "Fred, good luck. Serve well-chilled when we draw three million. POM."

Inside was a bottle of champagne. I still have that bottle in its original box.

We just missed the three-million mark that year, drawing 2,955,087, but the next year, we set an all-time attendance record of 3,347,845.

At the annual winter meetings in San Diego in December of 1986, Charles "Chub" Feeney announced he was stepping down as National League president. Peter was asked to lead a search committee to find a successor.

I was flattered when Peter informed me my name had been mentioned as a possible candidate. Peter felt it would be a conflict of interest for him to lead the committee if I had an interest in the position. I told Peter I had no interest in reporting to a group of owners. I wanted to report to only one owner and that was him.

The years had passed but our relationship had remained strong and candid. Peter opened the lunch by asking how my family was. Determined to be candid as always, I told him my family was hurt by my firing, and felt strongly that it was not deserved.

I also told Peter that, in my view, he shouldn't have been present at the firing. If he had asked for my advice, I would have told him to be a hundred miles away.

Better still, I said, he should have offered me a job that he knew I would turn down. Then, it wouldn't have been a firing on his part, but a decision on my part to leave. I felt this would have left the Dodgers in a better position and, to that extent, I was still thinking of what was best for the Dodgers.

Peter said he knew I wouldn't resign and that they would have to "blast me" out of my Dodger Stadium office. I conceded that was accurate.

I told Peter, in reply to his inquiry, I had no plans of returning to Dodger Stadium unless it was in a working capacity, either for a news organization or for another club. "I'll come back with another team to help beat the Dodgers if I have the opportunity," I said.

"Fred," Peter said, "the Fox people lost confidence in you on the Piazza deal."

I asked whether he meant the period leading up to the trade or my decision to be straightforward when the trade came down by revealing that I had nothing to do with it.

"Good question," said Peter, but he never gave me the answer.

Peter had provided the most honest explanation for my dismissal. Fox clearly wasn't pleased when I made it known the Piazza deal was something more than just a baseball trade. It was television business.

Prior to the trade, the Dodgers were projected to break even or be slightly in the black in 1998, according to Graziano. The Piazza trade increased the payroll $10 million and added nearly $100 million in future obligations. At that lunch, Peter told me the revised figures showed the Dodgers losing $15 million in 1998.

"You know," Peter said, "[*Times* sports editor] Bill Dwyre told me his newspaper has seldom received as many positive letters as it did about me when I announced the team was for sale. Isn't it strange that something like that has to happen before you receive recognition.

"Don't you think," he added, emotion clouding his voice, "that under different circumstances, I would have liked to have continued?"

CHAPTER XXIII

LIFE GOES ON

I became general manager of the Dodgers when Al Campanis was forced to resign in April of 1987.

I was fired on June 21, 1998, the day Al passed away.

And now here I was, five days after my firing, attending funeral services for him in Fullerton.

There were many Dodgers and former members of the organization in attendance. I found myself in the "former Dodger" category. It was a strange feeling after being a part of the organization for 30 years, but one overshadowed by the passing of a great friend.

It was an emotional day in many ways. When Sheryl and I drove to Fullerton, we knew we would encounter many friends for the first time since my firing.

I thought I had handled my dismissal as well as possible, holding a press conference at the Pasadena Ritz Carlton Huntington Hotel three days later.

With the day warm and beautiful, I must admit the occasion seemed more like a social gathering than a farewell appearance before the media. I was surrounded by family and friends. There were so many people in attendance who had been so supportive through the years. The event took the sting out of what had been labeled the "Sunday Night Massacre" by some of the media.

I thanked the Dodgers in general and the O'Malley family in particular for a wonderful opportunity.

When the press conference was over, Sheryl and I left the beautiful grounds of the Huntington Hotel to stop in at our favorite Pasadena hangout—Pie 'N Burger. Our lives were about to become a lot simpler, but hopefully just as enjoyable.

The one thing I didn't handle very well was the news I got that evening. I received a call from Dodger executive Charlie Blaney informing me that three Dodger coaches—pitching coach Glenn Gregson, bullpen coach Mark Cresse and hitting coach Reggie Smith—had been dismissed after the game against the Angels that night at Dodger Stadium.

All three had been called, one by one, into the office of interim manager Glenn Hoffman, with Tommy Lasorda present as the new general manager, to be given the shocking news.

And one by one, the trio left Hoffman's office and had to walk past the players to the opposite end of the clubhouse where the coaches' room is located.

I had never heard of a coach, let alone three coaches, being fired in such a manner. One veteran member of the organization told me it was the saddest day he had ever experienced in his baseball career. All three coaches had given many years of service to the Dodgers. They deserved a better fate. I was stunned and furious when I learned how the dismissals were handled.

When the services for Al were completed, people gathered outside the church.

Within a short time, I was approached by Tommy. "Fred," he said, "I just want you to know I had nothing to do with your firing."

"Tommy, I appreciate that, but," I said, my emotions boiling over, "I have to tell you, the way you handled the firing of those three coaches is one of the worst things I have ever seen in baseball."

"Well, how would you have done it?" Tommy countered.

"Tommy, you have every right to make whatever changes you want. But are you telling me, you couldn't have waited until the next day and called those coaches into your office one by one for a private meeting as opposed to doing it after the game?"

I had said what I had to say, but I recognized it figured to be one of the last times Tommy and I would be talking. Tommy is not one to forget such moments. But then, neither am I.

Tommy and I had a lot of great times together. I respect what he has contributed to baseball and to many good causes. I choose to think of the good times with him. I choose to think of the good times with the Dodgers.

And there were so many good times with so many wonderful people—the front office and staff people, the minor league personnel, the scouts, the players, the fans and, yes, the media. After all, that's where I had my start in baseball.

Other than to clean out my office, I haven't been back to Dodger Stadium with one exception. It's not that I'm bitter or upset. It's quite the opposite, in fact. I have so many great memories of being there and I want to keep those memories intact. You can't spend 30 years with a team without having great memories.

My one return trip to Dodger Stadium came when the team was out of town. It was in the summer of 2001 and I had just taken a position as a consultant for Performance Health Technologies of Boulder, Colo.

I wasn't sure how I could contribute to the company, but the one thing I knew is that the organization had great leadership in co-founders Dr. Michael Mellman and Marc Silverman. Both men encouraged me to join their group and I will always be grateful for that. The opportunity to be involved with a growing company came at just the right time.

The company has a shoulder rehab program and I wanted to visit the stadium to talk with Dodger physical therapist Pat Screnar and pitcher Darren Dreifort, who was using our shoulder device, called the SportsRAC.

It seemed strange to be at the stadium in a capacity other than as a Dodger executive. It was good to see some of the clubhouse guys, and I also ran into another Dodger pitcher who was doing rehab work, old friend Jesse Orosco.

I walked into the dugout and then onto the playing field and spent a few minutes under a warm sun, looking at the grounds that had been so familiar to me for so many years. I don't know if it was the glow of the sun or simply my deep feelings. I just knew it felt good to be in the stadium.

I know the time is near when I will go back to Dodger Stadium for games. Some of these things take time.

I have had more time for my family since my Dodger days. I was fortunate to have time to spend with my mother before she passed away from cancer at 88, the day after Mother's Day in 2000. She had fulfilled her desire to live to see 2000.

My love of sports was made possible by the guidance, encouragement and support I received from both of my parents. Of all the ballparks I ever entered, visiting Crosley Field in Cincinnati with my family remains my most memorable experience in baseball.

One of the things I wanted to do after I was fired was to teach. So I was thrilled when I received a wonderful opportunity at the University of Southern California to be a co-professor, along with my friend Jeff Fellenzer, of a class in the Annenberg School for Communication entitled, "Sports, Business and the Media in Today's Society."

But first, there was the matter of salary.

Fred and his son, Jeff.

"Fred," Jeff had warned me, "the people at the Annenberg School have told me they would like to have you involved, but there isn't much money in teaching a class like this."

Knowing Jeff had been given the responsibility for working out the details for my involvement, I told him, "Let's simplify this negotiation. You give me a figure and, whatever that figure is, I will say yes."

"You will?" Jeff said.

He gave me a salary figure and I immediately replied, "I accept, and I'm honored to be a part of USC."

The next day, I received a call from one of the school administrators, telling me I had just received the quickest raise in the history of USC.

Negotiations should have been so pleasant during my Dodger days.

I taught the class for three spring semesters, beginning in 1999. I now return several times a year to lecture.

Dealing with the students at USC has been a real treat. Both Jeff and I have been involved in placing a number of young people in the field of sports business. There's no more satisfying feeling than helping young people achieve their goals.

I've also been involved with the sports management graduate program at Cal State Long Beach as a member of the advisory board. It's a program conceived by former Dodger executive and longtime friend Bill Shumard, now the school's athletic director.

And I've been able to spend more time with the young people in my life—son Jeff and daughters Jennifer and Kimberly. I'm proud to say I'm also a grandfather, to Kyle and Katie, the two lovely children of Kim and her husband, Shane.

Fred with his daughters, Jennifer and Kim, at Dodgertown.

Fred and his wife, Sheryl, in the Summer of 2003.

The beautiful woman who was at my side for so many of my Dodger years remains at my side, my wife, Sheryl.

She was born and raised in Hanford, California—Giant territory. But when Sheryl and I met, her allegiance quickly turned to Dodger Blue. And the Dodgers never had a more loyal supporter. Neither have I, for that matter.

Both of us loved the competitive aspects of baseball. Our competitive drives are now focused on our golf game. Just ask the good folks at the Oakmont Country Club in Glendale, who see us walking the fairways regularly.

I also sneak in a little time for fly fishing.

I have been able to stay close to baseball with my consulting work with Performance Health and with a column I write on the sport for SportsTicker. But I realize I'm now at a distance from the game and the business that consumed me every waking hour.

I was playing golf at Oakmont one afternoon in April a couple of years ago with a friend of mine, Trent Merrick, when we suddenly heard and literally felt the jets that had zoomed over nearby Dodger Stadium.

"Oh, my gosh," I said to Trent, "it's opening day at Dodger Stadium."

I had been a part of planning those opening-day activities for three decades and now I had even forgotten they were occurring.

Yes, the game goes on. Life goes on.

Celebrate the Heroes of Baseball
in These Other Releases from Sports Publishing!

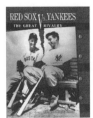